SOUTHAMPTON INSTITUTE

Southampton Institute Library Services Ltd
MOUNTBATTEN LIBRARY
Tel: (023) 80 319249
Please return this book no later than the last date stamped.
Loans may usually be renewed - in person, by 'phone, or
via the web OPAC.

ONE WEEK LOAN

2 4 JAN 2005		

First published in Great Britain in 1993 by
Allison & Busby
an imprint of Wilson & Day Ltd
5 The Lodge
Richmond Way
London W12 8LW

Typeset by TW Typesetting, Plymouth, Devon
Printed and bound in Great Britain by
Mackays of Chatham, Lordswood, Chatham, Kent

ISBN 0 7490 0161 5

CONTENTS

1

WHY RESEARCH FOR A NOVEL?

Sooner or later, anyone who attempts to write a novel will discover that research is something that cannot be avoided. The novel you intend to write may be the type you consider to be the easiest of all: written in contemporary style and period, from your own experience, and set in your own locality. But few of us can rely solely on our own memories, even for contemporary novels. Can you really remember with total accuracy any special events or disasters in any particular month of last year in your town? Or if your Town Hall really does have the adornments you say it does? Or at what time of the year it rained non-stop for nearly three weeks?

The majority of us would need to check reliable sources to find out any of these seemingly simple things. But your attention to accuracy and detail can make or break your novel in the eyes of your reader.

The novel you choose to write may be a densely plotted historical, or a crime novel involving police procedures, or one dealing in espionage. No professional author would dream of embarking on such themes without doing a considerable amount of research, both before and throughout the writing of the book. Even in the most fanciful story where the author creates a whole world out of his own imagination, some detail at least will need to be checked out, if only to make the whole thing read authentically.

The concept behind every novelist's work is to persuade the reader that what he is reading is real, and that the events could actually have happened. Therefore, however fantastic the story (for example, a science-fiction novel), considerable thought must be given to credibility. A fabulous new and intricate solar system may be invented by the author of such a novel, for instance. But without some reference to our own familiar solar system, if only to give our imaginations some yardstick, we can't identify quite so readily with the imaginary one.

You might argue that even if such a novel never had any actual reference to our own solar system, we have only to look at the sun and moon and stars to provide our own yardstick. Such parameters are universal, and we all have a basic knowledge of the things we can see and know. So why research . . .?

It's logical enough to say that if you have inside information on a subject, then you should use it. Dick Francis is a prime example of an author who knows a certain milieu (in his case the world of horse-racing) very well, and can therefore write with authority about it. I could not. Jeffrey Archer knows the world of politics. I do not. But if these subjects interested me enough to write about them, I would research them as thoroughly as I could, and hopefully produce a publishable novel. This is what research is all about.

Verifying the facts

To a novelist, research does not mean the same as it does to a journalist, a biographer or a historian. The novelist needs a solid background of factual information in which to weave his fictional story. He needs to make his fictional characters come alive in whatever time, place, vocation, class system or industry he places them. He needs to find out the many small facts which, when put together, will produce a rounded view of an era that is uniquely his own. And it's very often these small facts that enrich the novel more than anything else.

No one can argue that fact and fiction are inextricably intertwined in all walks of life, and from the earliest age. What child has not invented an imaginary friend to share his playtimes, and to take the blame when he is chastised! And is not the delightful imaginary playmate the child's alter-ego, the one into whose ears his very first story-telling experiences are poured?

It's a marvellous exercise to take a walk with a three-year-old and see the world through his eyes. He will see many things that the adult misses. A sense of place is created from the way he will describe things. He will examine in minute detail the shine of a leaf; laugh at the sound of a rooster, the plaintive bleat of a lamb, or the rush of a sudden breeze on still air; he will be fascinated by the movement of a tiny bug on the pavement, or the fragile wings of a hovering butterfly.

He will weave instant stories about these things too, for the instinctive art of story-telling is as old as time. But as we all know, stories get distorted in the telling, whether they are verbal or written down. And while a child's story-telling can reach fantastic heights, that's where the fantasy ends. In my opinion, an author who writes fiction without verifying facts is only doing half a job. And having checked, he should then take the time to double-check wherever possible, to make sure that the first source is accurate.

Not everything that is printed has been accurately recorded, and there are often discrepancies, even in the most seemingly esteemed research sources. In researching for one of my own books, I found conflicting records as to the relationship of a certain historical character to the central one. Was he a cousin or a nephew? Several of the books I checked had different opinions. I was anxious not to make an error over what was a historical fact, even though it was only for a small scene in the book, and the cousin/nephew wasn't going to appear again.

In the end, there was a simple solution. The book was set in Scotland, and I got around the problem by simply calling the man the hero's 'kinsman'. There are more ways than one of doing research, and of using it. You don't have to be hog-tied to a fact if you don't want to include it in your story, and there is often a simple way of getting around it.

User-friendly research

This book is intended for the enjoyment of novelists. I stress that point, because I think all research should be enjoyable, and not over-tedious. It advises browsing through the smallest handbook where you may pick up some useful tips. I won't list reference books of obscure origin, but hopefully will allow beginners, in particular, to find some research sources that are accessible and user-friendly. There may be ideas for research that you haven't considered before.

Nor will the book deal solely with finding out historical data, though obviously this is what most people think of in connection with research. But in all aspects of fiction writing, from biblical times to the present day, facts do need to be checked, locations need to be studied, and such basic things as weather conditions for documented events must be ascertained.

No reader should be told, for instance, that the Battle of Culloden took place on a warm sunny afternoon, when history records that in fact it happened in the early morning, and that the weather was dank and atrocious. Such a flaw in the writing immediately destroys the author's credibility in the eyes of the reader, who probably won't bother to pick up another book by the same writer.

The aim of this book is to share some of my own methods of researching, to offer some practical assistance, and to suggest some places to look for those elusive facts that flesh out your novels. To those who are still nervous of research, I can say that you are not alone. There was a time when I was very nervous of it too, but some sixty published novels later, I can say with certainty that it can be one of the most pleasurable parts of writing a novel, especially when the real hard work of sitting down and writing hasn't yet begun. Discovering some significant little fact that can lift a scene out of the ordinary into something perhaps unexpectedly exciting, yet perfectly logical, can be truly magical. And an interesting new fact, turned up while researching, can entirely change the direction of your novel.

And while this may be all to the good, it is also one of the pitfalls, especially if you've sent your publisher a detailed synopsis of your proposed novel. You may even have been given a contract on your original synopsis, and the editor may be less than pleased when an entirely new book shows up on his desk in a few months' time: your originally planned book may have been accepted, not only because of its good writing, but because it fitted well into the publisher's list. If you change it drastically, it may have inadvertently become too similar to another one already on the list, and you'll be back where you started. This is an extreme example, but it can happen, so always be careful not to get too carried away by your research and allow it to change the entire concept of your book. It is perilously easy to do.

Of course, if the above scenario doesn't apply to you, your researches may also give you the idea for a wonderful new novel, which will make your fortune . . . and I guarantee you'll be hooked on research from that time onwards.

Research should be fun

I enjoy research, and I think many novelists will endorse that feeling. I'm not denying that it can be hard work, but for me, the fun of it far outweighs the inconvenience.

I firmly believe in utilising those wise words from Rudyard Kipling. His 'six honest serving men' have long served me well in my writing career, and never more so than in the cause of research. They can apply to any kind of writing, but I include them now with my interpretation, especially for the novelist.

You should always be able to answer such questions clearly and positively, and keep them in mind throughout the writing. In the last chapter of this book, I will show in detail how I applied these questions, and my own research methods, in writing my First World War novel *The Bannister Girls*.

But back to Rudyard Kipling's famous six:

What are you actually writing about? (Theme and plot)
Why did the events in your story happen? (Motivation)
When did it all happen? (Dates/period/hour)
How did it all happen? (Your ingenious plotting)
Where did these things happen? (Location)
Who are you writing about? (Characters)

The human touch

The very idea of research undoubtedly stops some people from tackling a novel. Many people have told me they'd love to write a historical novel, for instance, 'but it's the thought of doing all that research . . .'

But despite all the necessary fact-finding, there's still one area that doesn't need the kind of detailed research that will be outlined in the following chapters, and that is the way people react to one another in any given situation. Human emotions don't change. Human nature is what it always was.

People who lived in the Stone Age had hopes and fears and needs as we do today, though in their case the very need to survive may have superseded all else. But this need, in turn, would have brought out all the greed, jealousy, hunting prowess, lusts and loves we can recognise, both in ourselves, and in characters throughout history. The entire range of human emotions and failings can be found just as easily in any Victorian or mediaeval novel as in a contemporary novel of the nineties.

So, unless you are totally without imagination, or unless your intention is to write a deeply psychological thriller, in which you will probably need to do some specialised research, you can forget about researching the inner feelings of people, because they are the same the world over, and throughout time.

It's just the remainder of the novel that you need to research. If that sounds a little facetious, it's merely to lighten the unfortunate fact that if you get something wrong in your novel, some sharp-eyed reader will usually spot it, even if it gets through the editorial net.

But don't be too despondent. Even Thomas Hardy got it wrong in *Tess of the D'Urbervilles*. He sent poor old Angel Clare off to Brazil, and had him nearly expiring of swamp fever in an area that was cool, dry, and healthy. Readers in Hardy's day were obviously not as well travelled as we are today, and were probably far less sophisticated in their reading, so they were less likely to spot such errors. But for your own integrity, for the editor's sanity, and if only to avoid your readers' fury, accuracy in research is essential.

Novels are about people, and in general, they are about ordinary people, though the novelist obviously needs to make the characters somewhat larger than life, if only to make them interesting to the reader. It's pointless to write about people who lead such dull lives that nobody could care less what happens to them.

By 'ordinary people' I mean the ones like you and me, and without belittling either of us, I'm comparing us with those who have got into the history books, such as Joan of Arc and Field-Marshal Montgomery. Or members of the Royal Family, or the Pope, or noted stars of stage and screen . . . well, you see what I mean. So the novelist needs to get inside the lives of the ordinary people he will use as prototypes for his characters and find out what makes them tick. Whether your hero is a latter-day spy or a mediaeval knight; or your heroine is a nurse serving with Florence Nightingale, or a juke-box attendant at an amusement park, you need to get into the minds of these people and know just how they live their daily lives. That's what you need to research.

And into the lives of these ordinary people will inevitably come others. Your characters may well come into contact with some noted personality. They may be involved in events far removed from their normal lives, such as wars or riots, or crewing for Oxford, or being invited to a Buckingham Palace garden party, or to Ascot. You may decide to send your characters to Spain for a holiday, or on safari to Kenya.

Ideas for novels can come thick and fast, and putting a workable story together is what a novelist's imagination is all about. But the more ambitious the story, the sooner you arrive at the point where the imagination ends and you realise that the research has to begin.

An overall look at research

Among other research sources, I will be detailing many reference books and materials in the following chapters. A good number of them are in my own collection, and although some of the books are of a good size and price, many of them are no more than pamphlets and brochures that can be picked up at any holiday resort. I want to emphasise that it needn't cost a fortune to build up your own library of research books and ephemera. Nor do you need a mansion to keep them all in.

I will also show how and where I find the facts I need for prospective novels, and for those in progress, and the way in which just finding an interesting piece of research material can trigger off the idea that results in a successful novel. It's happened many times over for me, and it can do so for you.

For those just beginning to write for publication and perhaps thinking that the whole idea of research is too much, I want to take a few moments listing some of the things I've written about in my own novels. I especially want to point out that, with one or two exceptions, I knew next to nothing about any of the following subjects until I researched them, but all of them, and many more, have ended up in published novels. My subjects include: the Jacobite Rebellion, the American Civil War, the Indian Mutiny, the Crimean War, the First and Second World Wars, female emigration to Australia in 1834, the Great Exhibition of 1851, the San Francisco earthquake of 1906, the Bristol Riots of 1831, the 1920s and the General Strike.

Industries and activities include: nineteenth-century willow-growing, basket-making and cider-making, Australian sheep-farming, Aborigine burial grounds, seventeenth-century piracy off the African coast, nursing in nineteenth-century battle hospitals, Spanish bull-fighting, Scottish antiques, Cornish wreckers, gypsy customs, Yorkshire wool production, Cornish china-clay production, tea-planting in nineteenth-century Ceylon, gold-mining in California, nineteenth-century Tunisian desert tribes, witchcraft, pot-holing, pop festivals.

Historical figures include: Queen Victoria and Prince Albert,

Abraham Lincoln, Florence Nightingale, Isambard Kingdom Brunel and Bonnie Prince Charlie.

Know what you're writing about

I'm no genius to have written about all these things, and I certainly had no idea before I started each book how easy or how difficult it was going to be to research its subject and setting. But each topic was a challenge, and I researched them all very well. And I have to admit, that once I've finished a book I usually forget most of the research I've done for it, because by then I'm thinking about the next one.

But I hope the above information bears out a phrase I've always upheld as being a good stand-by. This is not the more popular, and perfectly valid one, *Write about what you know*, but my own version of it, which is *Know what you're writing about.*

I was once a guest on a local TV programme, and one of the other guests was a well-known lady novelist. While we were sitting around for the inevitable hours they make you wait before the rehearsal, let alone going on air, I was impressed by the way she was making copious notes about the various studio procedures and personnel. She must have been in a TV studio dozens of times, but she didn't miss the chance of taking advantage of that particular situation, and her research resulted in a best-selling novel.

The authority that comes from your own inner knowledge of your subject will show through in the writing, even if you end up only using a fraction of what you've learned. Like the tip of the iceberg, only a tiny portion of your research may show, but all the rest of it will be forming a good solid base beneath the surface. And it will all have been worth it. With all that inner knowledge giving substance to your writing, no one will doubt the credibility of *your* book.

To me, that's the whole crux of what makes research so fascinating and worthwhile, and such fun. But be warned: it can also be addictive. There's always a danger in getting so wrapped up in research that you forget that your real purpose is in finding out facts for your novel – and actually writing it. But that's all part of the pleasure and satisfaction it brings, because if *you're* totally absorbed in what you're discovering, the chances are that your readers will be too.

And you never know quite where you're going to find these great snippets of information. Some of the best research can arise quite accidentally, over a chat in the local pub, for instance, or finding an intriguing name in a country churchyard. So never forget to take out your notebook or tape recorder or camera – or maybe all three – and embark on what I think is one of the novelist's most enjoyable journeys: research.

Starter information

To whet your appetite, I want to suggest some of the minor and extremely cheap ways of doing preliminary research. But I must stress that this is the preliminary research, and would lead you on to doing further and more detailed research. Just as novelists need to flesh out their characters, you will also need to flesh out your facts.

Looking around your own town is a quick and easy way of researching a possible locality for a novel, or a place on which to base a fictitious one. And how often we forget the obvious! Going no farther than your own beach, high street or local factory can provide you with a location, architectural style or background right away.

Old postcards can show you dress styles, moods of an era, even the language favoured at the time. I shamelessly copied into one of my novels the style of the gown and the pretty hair decorations on a lovely postcard that was once sent to my mother, and used the sentiments of the writer as a guide to the endearments of letter-writers of that time.

And do you remember those lovely silk postcards of yesteryear? Imagine your historical heroine's emotions on receiving one of those, and you're already halfway to imagining the scene, and the circumstances, and the sender . . .

Posters can be a rich source of information. The idea for one of my novels began with a poster I saw in a museum in Melbourne, Australia. It gave a great deal of detail about the British government's sponsored emigration passage to Australia in 1834, and when I studied it with my novelist's eyes, I could immediately see the potential in such an adventure.

I asked the museum assistant if I could buy a copy of the poster for research purposes, and stated the reason. The poster wasn't for sale, alas, but the museum assistants were excited to think that a writer might be able to use something from their museum in a novel. They did a gratis photocopy of the poster for me. This led me to research the Australian outback, resulting in my novel *Outback Woman* (Sally Blake, Mills & Boon Masquerade).

Remember those old cigarette cards that used to be so collectable? There was a mass of information contained on the back of them, whether it was about footballers, aeroplanes or whatever. How many of us have thrown them away carelessly, never dreaming of their potential as starter information for a novel. It's not only historical things that need researching. Hadn't you forgotten how long those footballers' 'shorts' used to be in the not-so-distant past?

In mentioning all these things, I hope that by now your own imagination is getting into gear and reminding you of some of the things you'd half forgotten. All those old mementoes you have in your attic or basement, for instance; the old school photographs reviving memories of what it was like in the forties, fifties, sixties or whenever; the old photographs of the Anderson and Morrison shelters during the Second World War, and the utility clothes we/they wore; the make-do-and-mend, the dried eggs and clothing coupons.

If you're lucky enough to own any antiques, handed down to you by parents or grandparents, they could well be looked at with new eyes. Can you see the potential in weaving a story around them? And all this under your own roof! How did your family acquire them? What is their history? Why did a dealer offer to pay such a high price for them? I promise it takes little to spark you off, once you get your novelist's imagination working.

Keeping it all in order

If you're not a collector already, I guarantee that any novelist keen on research will become one. And as your own collection of books, papers, brochures, et cetera grows, you will need to devise some system of keeping everything in order. Books are easy enough, providing you have enough shelves to keep them on, but small things can be easily lost. I tend to keep material on various subjects in packet folders, each labelled accordingly. Thus I have many brochures from Cornish locations in one large folder, and brochures of big country houses in another.

If there are very small items, then see-through plastic envelopes tell me at a glance that I have entry tickets from certain places (useful for price references, opening times et cetera), photographs, and so on. I put newspaper cuttings into plastic envelopes, and then into a labelled clip-file. A box-file is useful if you like the things, but whatever you do, it's less time-consuming to begin your own system as soon as possible, and to stick to it. Even an old shoe-box can be used.

Label everything as you go along, and get into the habit of pencilling lightly on the backs of photographs the date, place and time they were taken. Or, to lessen the risk of marking the photos, stick labels with the same information on the backs. Wedding photos are a good way of keeping up with the times and styles – or going back to times past.

Finally, make a note of each source, particularly when using reference books, whether they are your own, or library borrowings. Note the title, author and page number where you found your required information, and keep it on a separate list. If you don't, it's quite likely you'll have completely forgotten your source when you want to add to it, or do a double-check.

At the end of each of the following chapters is a list of relevant reference books, and/or places to visit. These can never be fully comprehensive lists, but are intended as guides to the kind of research sources available. Many of the books are ones that I own, or I have visited the places I've mentioned and can personally recommend them. A starter shortlist follows of some series of books, as opposed to individual titles. Some are children's books, some are light-hearted but informative. All are useful for research.

Bluffers' Guides, The
Foyles Handbooks
Hamlyn Little Guides, The
Key Facts, The (and similar series of GCSE revision notes)
Ladybird Books, The
Observer Books, The
Shire Publications – inc. Discovering Books, Shire Albums, Lifelines (potted biographies)
V & A Museum, The, Arts and Living series (HMSO).

2

GENERAL RESEARCH SOURCES

When did it first happen?

One of the first things to establish in any novel is when the action took place. Apart from getting absorbed in the lives of the characters in the book, the time in which the story is set is one of the first things the reader wants to know.

In its broadest form, settings can be divided into two main types. Is it a contemporary novel or a historical one? Within those two over-simplified sections come the many sub-divisions, because the things that happened in 1920 will be vastly out of date by the forties or even the thirties. As for the present decade, the inventions and procedures of years before will seem practically archaic. Similarly, the artefacts that seemed so progressive in the Industrial Revolution will be museum pieces now. Nor is it any use having a nostalgic memory for some old kitchen relic your great-grandmother may have passed down to you, and deciding to include it in your novel, if the relic went back to the early late 1890s, and was obsolete by 1910. So, while it's pretty obvious that you will be aware of the date in which you set your own novel, it's not always so obvious to establish that the things you describe were around and in use at the time.

Dictionaries and encyclopaedias

Everyone has a dictionary on their shelves, and many contain date references. The *Oxford English Dictionary* gives the earliest dates in which many words are used. In the 1840s, for instance, the word 'crinoline' was in use, but it meant petticoats lined with stiff horsehair cloth. The metal crinoline wasn't introduced until 1856. Net and tarlatan cloth were new textiles in 1840.

And beware of giving your hero a beard before 1860. Of course, men wore them, but they weren't considered respectable until that time. *Punch* magazine made fun of the beard-and-moustache movement in 1853, when it was difficult for men to shave during the Crimean War.

Some other excellent research sources are the *Hutchinson Encyclopaedia*, *Pears*, *Brittanica Book of the Year*, and the indispensible Whitaker's *Almanac*. If you haven't discovered Whitaker's yet, then you're missing out on a treat, since it contains the who, how, when, what and whether of the present time and is an amazing source of contemporary detail.

What do you need to know?

Historical novelists establish their settings quickly, and rightly so. It's important to get your readers into the mood and background of your book. The very first pages will undoubtedly have reference to things of the past, be they gas-lighting or oil lamps, rush matting on the floor, or bedding made from horse-hair – whatever is relevant to the time period of the book.

Quite possibly, some kind of horse-drawn vehicle will come flying through the night, flamboyantly named as a post-chaise, or a stage-coach, or a hansom cab. And unless the author has checked on the era in which all of these things first came into use and, just as significantly, went out again, the book will be doomed in the eyes of the knowledgeable reader (and the editor).

Of course you can always invent places and ceremonies . . . one author invented such a beautiful and original wedding ceremony in an imaginary American location that an American lady wrote to ask her where it was, since she wanted to photograph the place. That was good writing, and inventing can be fun.

But you will inevitably need to check on certain facts, and even though much of your actual research may form only a minuscule part of your book, it still needs to be accurate. Even verifying a tiny but vital fact can take up a great deal of your time. Research *is* time-consuming.

You can spend hours browsing through books in a library, for instance, and end up getting nowhere. So you need to weigh up the value of every piece of research than you undertake. There are always days when you almost stumble on something that is immensely useful for your book, and others when you feel frustrated at every turn.

My own research for a novel is continuous. It begins with the initial concept of my book, and continues all the time I am writing it until the very last page. I don't gather up everything needed for a novel, spending perhaps six months or a year on the research before spending a similar amount of time writing the book. But this may well work for you, and whichever method suits each individual novelist best is obviously the one to follow.

But because I am a novelist first and a researcher second, I think I would have lost interest in my subject long before such lengthy and non-productive (in terms of manuscript pages written) research were up. Once I have my relevant background and enough details to begin, I always long to get on with my book. I need to see those first chapters take shape, so my research time is interwoven with my writing time and becomes less cumbersome. It is not so much a chore as a delight.

Finding out when things first happened, when they were invented, when they were fashionable or went out of date, is one of the fascinations of research. On my bookshelf I have an invaluable book called *The Shell Book of Firsts*, by Patrick Robinson, published by Ebury Press and Michael Joseph. My edition was published in 1983, and here I must say that many of my own well-used reference books are quite likely to be out of print. I include them because of their value to me and their likely value to other novelists. Out-of-print books can often be tracked down in libraries and second-hand bookshops, or can be borrowed from friends.

I frequently refer to *The Shell Book of Firsts* as a reference guide. Within its pages I can check when the first aeroplane was equipped with radio, when the first elastic bands were patented, when the first marriage bureau came into use, the date of the first mail-order business, the first parking meter. With date, place and charges included, I discover (if I needed to know it) that the first television panel game was the six-a-side *Spelling Bee*, compered by Freddie Grisewood and broadcast on 31 May 1938. I note that the first woman to wear trousers was Sarah Bernhardt in 1876.

As well as these 'firsts', there is a lot of detail concerning the subject, all of which can be a starting point for further research. One of the many things I've discovered in my own researches is that one thing can lead you on to other sources, sometimes quite effortlessly. If you want to know when the first women's magazine was published, its name, its content, and style of reporting, then you'll find it in *The Shell Book of Firsts*, together with other fascinating details concerning magazine publishing. And one vital, but important piece of information is surely when the first zip-fastener came into being. And when was the first safety-pin used? Chronological data is given at the end of the book, covering many diverse and varied subjects.

Another volume which I've found just as useful is the *Dunlop Book of Facts*. My edition was compiled by the McWhirter brothers in 1966, and covers a wider-ranging table of contents than the Shell book. On a broader scale, you can find anything you need to know regarding world physical geography and the physical and political geography of the UK, as well as historical and constitutional information – but obviously only until 1966 in this particular volume. It's useful for finding out about UK coinage, Orders of Merit, the order of succession, and so on. If you need to know the world's tallest, highest, lowest, largest, or deepest, the *Dunlop Book of Facts* is also your source. The sciences are dealt with in some detail, and there are lists of sporting achievements, information on civil and criminal juris-diction, the arts, and defence data, both world and UK.

This is just the kind of book to give you a basic grounding in your researches, but in most instances you will need to dig deeper to obtain greater detail. But it does what it sets out to do, and gives you the facts. I recommend it for its quick reference value, and similar volumes would be useful additions to any novelist's bookshelf.

Others are *The Pan Book of Dates*, and the marvellous *Chronicle of the 20th Century*. Now this *is* expensive, at almost £30, but worth every penny, in my opinion. You could do as I did, and get it for a Christmas present. This particular book gives you a day-by-day, month-by-month rundown of the main events during the whole of the century up to the end of 1987. It's written in easy-to-read newspaper-style reporting, with many illustrations, and I defy anyone to browse through it without coming up with an idea for a novel. Though be warned: it's far too heavy to hold on your knees without seriously impeding the blood supply. There are other useful books in the same series, notably *Chronicle of America*.

Basic research sources

I hardly need to mention the library as being a basic research source. Make a friend of your local librarian. Interest her in your project, and she will go to endless trouble for you. My local librarians take a great interest in knowing that I write books, and are always intrigued if I take out half a dozen books on the one subject, rightly suspecting that this is what my next novel will be about.

They have also obtained reference books for me from other parts of the country, including a rare book from the Edinburgh History Society for study within the library premises. In the main town library we also have an excellent reference department, where books are intended more for serious study than for the enjoyment of mere reading. Once you become a researcher for your own work, those days have a habit of disappearing, for everything will now be looked at with an eye to research, and 'finding out'.

The children's library is an excellent place in which to start any research. Research for my book *Scarlet Rebel* began with a Ladybird book called *Bonnie Prince Charlie*. It detailed Charles Stuart's sojourn in Britain so clearly and illustratively that it was a perfect starting point.

Another children's book I found useful is written in the form of a novel. It details a young English boy's long summer holiday with a Dutch family, and how he learned their way of life and became absorbed into it. Much of the information it contains, together with travel brochures, maps and further reading in the adult library, formed the backbone of one of my later contemporary novels.

There are major well-known libraries in this country, such as the British Library in London or the Bodleian Library in Oxford, but every large town and city will have adequate facilities for most novelists.

To those who live well out of London and the Home Counties, and who require specialist information on any subject, I suggest you talk to your own librarian for further contacts.

Old newspapers and archives

The invaluable British Library Newspaper Library has a wealth of material for the novelist who has the time and opportunity to visit it. Its collection of newspapers and useful data is immense. We're fortunate in that Victorian reporters, in particular, took an almost lascivious delight in recording speeches of the day by such eminents as national and local politicians.

You will also find accounts of openings of canals, schools, hospitals and other places of interest. Victorians especially loved sensational stories about murderers and other criminals, and where better to find them than in first-hand accounts of the times?

Old newspapers are a great source of information, not just for finding out what happened on a certain day and date, but also for the weather, the style of language prevalent at the time through reported dialogue, the fashions contained in the advertisements, prices for clothes, medicines and so on, as well as what films, concerts, theatre productions, and television programmes, if any, were appearing on any given date.

Some years ago a series of reprinted newspapers called *The War Papers* was on sale at newsagents. They were a wonderful source of information for novelists researching the Second World War, and built up into a comprehensive documentary of events and procedures. They included maps, posters, details of uniforms on both sides, weaponry, armaments and so on. Although out of print now, they may be worth a search in a second-hand bookshop that also sells old newspapers.

Your own local newspaper archives can provide you with local historical information, and many newspapers nowadays reprint articles from the past, including what happened locally 25, 50 and 100 years ago. Such snippets gives a rounded picture of the times, prices, and events in your area, and are the kind of thing well worth collecting and filing.

On reaching a certain birthday, one of my most welcome gifts was an edition of *The Times* published on the day I was born. It makes fascinating reading, and is a source of rich detail about that particular time.

A bookshop simply called Books, in a small backstreet in Ilfracombe in Devon, sells old newspapers and magazines, mainly from the 1950s. The recent past is an area where many novelists can easily slip up. We think we remember it so well, but a glance through some of those old magazines reminds you how life was then; what clothes cost then; and how amazingly naive we seemed to be, even in so short a time-span back from today.

Second-hand bookshops are a joy to the researching novelist. They exist in most towns, but the mecca for those who have found it has to be Hay-on-Wye near Hereford. The town is practically taken over by one enormous second-hand bookshop area, and many of the shops have sections devoted to various kinds of research books. I have spent many absorbing days there, and hope to do so again. Some of the 'finds' are cheap, though many are not, but as a research source the whole town is second to none.

My library, like many others, holds a second-hand book sale several times a year, when many unwanted books are offered for sale at ridiculously low prices. This again is something to watch out for, as are car boot sales and markets. You can often pick up a really good book or magazine bargain there.

Book clubs can provide many cheap editions of suitable

research books, but can eventually become very expensive if you're committed to buying a certain number of books throughout the year, many of which are of no further use to you. Actually, I've found that this doesn't happen as often as you might think, since a good proportion of book-club lists are made up of non-fiction books. But you need to be selective, to know what you're buying – and to take advantage of the cheap come-on offers to get the best value. For me, that also means buying the kind of book that you can use over again.

Published books are an obvious source of research, but as well as using any factual information contained in them, always check any bibliography at the end. This will give you the names of similar books that you may find just as useful, or even more so, than the original one.

Theme parks, TV and films

In recent years, theme parks have proved to be one of my favourite new research sources. They exist everywhere now, from Flambards in Cornwall, with its marvellous reconstruction of a Victorian town, its authentic Blitz scenario, Battle of Britain war gallery and Aero Park, to Eden Camp near Malton in Yorkshire, again with reconstructions of Second World War scenes. Eden Camp includes a 'visit inside a submarine', with eerie sonar soundings and greenish sea water outside the supposed sub, with a 'drowned' diver floating endlessly by.

In Cornwall you can go down a tin mine at the Geevor Tin Mines, visit Frontier City, purported to be the original 1880s Wild West town, visit the Charlestown Shipwreck and Heritage Centre or find out all about the Cornish goldsmiths at the National Gold Centre near Portreath.

You are invited to experience the nostalgia of a bygone age

at the Trereife Farm Park at Penzance, where you can find out all about gypsy life as well as visiting a historic house.

Such places aren't confined to Cornwall. Beamish Open Air Museum in Durham is a reconstruction theme park, as is Morwellham Quay in Devon. And for getting right back to Viking times, there's the Jorvik Viking Exhibition in York.

There are many more such places, and all can be used to great effect for visually aiding your research. (Relevant ones will be detailed in later chapters.) As an extra bonus, the inevitable gift shops also include useful books and booklets on the topic of the theme park, and quite frequently, those old reprinted newspapers pertinent to the times.

TV documentaries are a relatively new source of research information for novelists. They crop up regularly, but for those people who own a video machine, documentary video films can also be hired. They cover practically any subject, and can be watched at leisure in your own home, paused for notes to be taken, and re-run as many times as you wish. If you can't visit the real place or see the craftsmen at work, there's nothing like the visual impact of a film to bring a subject to life.

And even those old Hollywood films shouldn't be despised as rubbish. Maybe Hollywood's version of the Second World War or ancient Rome wasn't always exactly true to life, but it can still give us a flavour of those times. If the subject interests us enough and we decide to investigate further through some more authentic historical work, then the film will have served a useful purpose, especially if it results in a published novel. Even some of the old silent films that we laugh at today can evoke a vivid picture of what life was like then.

If you have the time and inclination, a visit to the Museum of the Moving Image in London is well worth while. You have the whole story of moving pictures here from pre-cinema days to the latest hologram technology. From the silent cinema section to 'hands-on' experiences such as making your own cartoons in an animation workshop, there is a whole new world for you to utilise as a novel background.

Ask the man who knows

If you're still struggling to find out the facts, why not go straight to the expert? There is always someone who can provide the information you need, if you know who to ask for it. Information centres to help you with locations, maps, museums et cetera are everywhere.

The Citizens' Advice Bureau can put you in touch with local organisations or national ones. The addresses of local businesses or factories can be found in the Yellow Pages of the telephone directory, and the press or publicity officer of a company will probably assist you with details of his or her organisation.

Contact any of the social services, such as police, fire or ambulance, for any relevant information, though it's always advisable to write to them in the first instance. You may well be invited in to observe procedures, or at least be sent various pamphlets to study at leisure.

Embassies and diplomatic consulates all have their press departments, and the press officer is the one to write to with queries. Always send large stamped addressed envelopes, and be prepared to wait for a reply if necessary.

Writing to specific firms will often produce a great mass of information and historical background, and they can be quite overwhelming in their wish to oblige. Remember that you may well be doing them a favour by mentioning their firm in your novel, or by giving them an acknowledgement for their help in your preface. They, as well as you, will want their product or industry portrayed accurately. So it's worth keeping that point in mind while politely requesting information, and you won't do yourself any harm in tactfully mentioning it to them.

Novelists of my acquaintance have variously contacted Clarks, for information in the shoe-making industry; a millinery firm; Smirnoff Vodka for details into its history and background, and so on. Experts are always willing to talk or write to you about their work, providing you approach them with courtesy and show that you appreciate their time and knowledge. One may not always think of the tax inspector as a friend, but who better to contact if you need to know the rate of income tax in the twenties or thirties?

But there may be experts far nearer home than you think. We all have friends, relatives and acquaintances with a wealth of knowledge about a great diversity of subjects. Look around you, and discover them. Enlist your friends to supply you with any information they may have on your subject, or theirs. They may not have direct information to give you, but, as the TV advert says, they may well know a man who does . . .

By chance I discovered that the father of a friend used to be a basket-maker, and could give me details of a craftsman's personal working methods that I hadn't been able to find out any other way, despite visiting the Somerset basket-makers myself.

When all else fails, you might even try something else I did in the name of research. For that same book, *Willow Harvest* (Rowena Summers, Sphere and Severn House), I especially wanted to know how the withies (the Somerset name for the willows) smelled when they were boiled for the basket-making process, and I couldn't seem to find out. So, having a weeping willow tree in the garden, I reasoned that willows were willows, brought an armful of them into the kitchen, and boiled them up in a large saucepan. Unfortunately, there was no wonderful aromatic or pungent smell I could describe. They smelled only of steam – but at least I now confidently knew that, and the neighbours probably had a field day, wondering just what witches' brew I was cooking up.

More adventurously, a certain lady novelist I know, wanting absolute accuracy for her next novel, went up in a hot air balloon just to get the feel of it. Now, that's what I call dedication.

Following on loosely from that, your contemporary novel may contain some reference to a specific airline, and also many details about the aeroplane itself. How important are these details to the reader? Maybe not at all, but if you have made a point of naming the airline, perhaps stating that the seats were pale grey, and that the stewardesses wore red uniforms, you had better be right.

One simple way to get around all this is to invent your own airline, and then you have a free rein. Beginners seem extraordinarily nervous of doing such a thing, but there must be more invented towns, cities, streets, businesses, shops, islands and other worlds than could ever be researched. The secret is to make them *seem* real, and you do this by giving them such an authentic ring that the reader is never quite sure whether or not you are writing about a real place or a fictional one.

But back to the airline quoted above. If you really do want to quote a certain airline, and you think that its interior decor and the dress colours of the stewardesses is integral to your story, then you have various options.

You can write to the publicity officer of the airline concerned, asking them for information, stating that you are an author and that you are very keen to mention their airline in your book. Everyone likes flattery, and publicity material is almost guaranteed.

Or you can go to any travel agent, find a brochure featuring flights by that airline, and check it out. The chances are there will be photographs of the friendly airline staff, and there may just be photographs of the interior of the plane. If not, ask any of the travel agency staff if they have used this airline, and what it was like inside the plane. They may not be as observant as you would wish them to be, but then, they probably weren't researching a novel at the time of their flight.

You may have friends who have used the airline, or are about to do so. Enlist their help. They will probably also be flattered that you have asked them to do this for you. And if you're a reticent author (and there are some), it may be easier on your nerves to get your information through a third person.

Finally, you could always take a trip on the airline yourself, and put it down to research expenses for the tax man. This is not as tongue-in-cheek as it sounds, because research expenses are quite legitimate. And what could be nicer than being able to justify the expense by quoting the title and content of your new book to the tax inspector, if he queries it?

As a final addition to this chapter, *Bibliophile* is a marvellous postal remainder shop, which issues a regular catalogue of bargain books at remainder prices. Address below.

Sources relevant to this chapter

Books (pub. date given where known)

Bonnie Prince Charlie, Ladybird Books.
Brittanica Book of the Year
Chronicle of America, Longman, 1989.
Chronicle of Britain, Longman, 1992.
Chronicle of the 20th Century, Longman, 1988.
Dunlop Book of Facts, 1966.

Everyman's Dictionary of Dates, Audrey Butler, Dent, 1971.

Facts About an Airline, André Deutsch.

Facts About a Feature Film, Marjorie Bilbow, André Deutsch, 1978.

Facts About a Theatre Company, André Deutsch.

Forty Years in Hollywood, Castle Books, New York, 1971.

Guinness Book of Film Facts and Feats

Guinness Book of Records – annually.

Hollywood, When Silents Were Golden, Evelyn F. Scott, McGraw-Hill, USA, 1972.

Hutchinson Encyclopaedia, The

Oxford English Dictionary

Pears Cyclopaedia, annually

Professional Filmmaking, Tab Books, USA, 1974.

Shell Book of Firsts, The, Ebury Press, 1983.

Teach Yourself Encyclopaedia of Dates and Universal Information, L. C. Pascoe, EUP, 1974.

Whitaker's Almanac, Whitaker, London, annually.

Places to visit

Beamish Open Air Museum, nr Chester-le-Street, Durham.

Charlestown Shipwreck and Heritage Centre, St Austell, Cornwall.

Geevor Tin Mines, Cornwall.

Eden Camp, nr Malton, North Yorkshire.

Flambards, nr Helston, Cornwall.

Frontier City, nr St Columb Major, Cornwall.

Jorvik Viking Exhibition, York.

Morwellham Quay, nr Tavistock, South Devon.

National Gold Centre, nr Portreath, Cornwall.

Trereife Farm Park, Penzance, Cornwall.

Other

Bibliophile Books, 21 Jacob Street, London SE1 2BG.
Bodleian Library, Oxford.
British Library and Newspaper Library, Colindale Avenue, London NW9 5HE.
The War Papers.

3

THE TRAPPINGS OF ORDINARY PEOPLE

What did they wear?

In any novel, the characters need to be dressed in the appropriate attire of their time, status and profession or calling. Fleshing out the characters means that at some time or other you will need to describe their clothes, hairstyles, and general appearance, both to paint a picture of them for your readers, and to make them more believable to yourself.

There are many books on costume and fashion available, and one of the most useful I have found is *Costume and Fashion 1760–1920* by Jack Cassin Scott, Blandford Press. This book is not only beautifully illustrated in full colour, but also gives thorough descriptions of the clothes pictured. There are also black and white sketches, and details of many clothing terms relevant to each period.

A book on similar lines is *Dressed To Impress, 1840–1914* by Christina Walkley, Batsford. Another one, which covers a far longer span, is *A Concise History of Fashion* by James Laver, BCA. There are many other such books to be found in libraries, and many enjoyable hours can be spent browsing through them in the name of research. Accuracy in dress is important, since styles change so quickly.

You can often come across the information you need by accident. When researching for my book *Scarlet Rebel*, set in the Jacobite Rebellion, I found all the details of Bonnie Prince Charlie's dress and appearance, together with other Scottish tartans and clan badges, in a history of Scottish clans and tartans in the reference section of my local library. I wasn't looking for such detail at the time, but it contributed to what I needed.

If your novel is about a specifically short period, such as the Regency, you will need to find specialised sources. In the 'Costume in Context' series, GCSE History List, you will find *The Regency*, *The 1940s* and *The 1950s*, for instance, by Jennifer Ruby, Batsford. A day spent in any of the wonderful costume galleries in a museum such as the York Museum will give you instant visual impressions of the formal and informal clothes people wore at certain periods.

For more official and ritual styles of dress, most of the stately homes open to the public also have costume galleries. The Bowes Museum, at Barnard Castle in Yorkshire, houses the Queen Elizabeth Gallery of Costume, covering photos and detail from George II to George V. The brochure I bought there, showing most of the range, cost me 25 pence. The Assembly Rooms, Bath, has another excellent display, and Kensington Palace in London has an exhibition of court dress from 1750 onwards.

The full title of the display at the Bath Assembly Rooms is the Museum of Costume and Fashion Research Centre. There are study facilities there, and there is also a postal enquiry service. Write to the Keeper of Costumes at the address below for further details.

Serious novelists rarely travel without a notebook or camera, though many times these are the very things you forget! Interior photographs are often not allowed, especially in stately homes; flash photography would damage the fragile embroideries or colours, just as sunlight does, which is why we so often have to view the rooms with curtains drawn. So be prepared to buy either the complete brochure of the place you are visiting, or one of the smaller brochures, covering the period you need. If money is really tight, buy a postcard. If you don't take advantage at the time of your visit, the chances are you'll never remember quite the image you need to describe in your novel. I speak from experience.

Even if the initial layout is more than I could really afford, I've tried to splash out on a certain amount of memorabilia. Keep in mind that all research material is claimable on your income-tax returns, even if you haven't yet used it. 'Work in progress' is in the head as much as on paper, and if you're earning enough to pay income tax, then you can be considered a serious novelist who needs to research. And research has to be done before the finished article, the published novel, can be produced.

Getting up to date

For fashion and style covering the first half of the twentieth century, Cecil Beaton's *The Glass of Fashion*, Cassell, is an excellent reference book. But we often ignore the obvious in our research. Something as simple as a browse around a department store will show you what's in today, and any mail-order catalogue will keep even the housebound author right up to the minute in describing your characters' clothes, hairstyles and jewellery. It's well worth sending for one of these catalogues for this purpose alone.

Contemporary television programmes, not forgetting children's programmes, will also keep you up to date in fashion. Kids are very fashion-conscious these days, and to dress your junior character in the wrong style for the period will only annoy readers. This applies especially if you're writing teenage novels. The fad for specialised training shoes, for instance, has a lot to answer for, and so does television advertising, so make full use of them both for your research.

The easiest way of all to research is surely by observing what we see around us every day. Watch what people are wearing when you travel by bus, plane or train. Taking notes can help to pass the time (unless you're the driver), and so can taking photographs of people on holiday, or at functions, or just going about their everyday work.

Could you instantly describe a British Rail guard's uniform, for instance? I certainly couldn't, yet I must have seen one many times. I can picture an airline pilot, but I couldn't say exactly what he was wearing. Does it matter? If it affects your story, then it does. If it doesn't why bother?

Weekly or monthly magazines are an obvious way of keeping up with the fashion times without any great outlay. I don't necessarily mean such specialised or sophisticated ones as *Vogue*, but the regular ones that appear on the bookshelves every week. They all have a fashion and beauty section.

The New Look covers fashion, entertainment, national events et cetera in the postwar period from 1947 onwards. *The People's Chronology* schedules events from earliest times, and covers an enormous range of data and information.

I have no experience with science-fiction writing, so as far as dressing such characters is concerned, I can offer no help. But since no one can predict what fashions in the distant future will be like, I suggest that you either refer to those books and magazines already on the market, or resort to your own instincts and imagination. Personally, I think that would be much more fun.

The twenties

This is an era I have much enjoyed writing about, and I include it particularly, because nostalgia is so in with novelists these days and the twenties were a vastly entertaining and evolving time.

The period between wars is always a time of change, development and new thinking, and perhaps never more than after the First World War, with the ensuing flu epidemic that ravaged the country, and the emergence into a new decade. Added to this came the jazz age, the Charleston, movie madness, Oxford bags, and then the General Strike which paralysed the general exuberance of the country. All the ingredients for the background for a novel seem to be encapsulated in that turbulent and exciting decade.

That was the way I saw it when I set *To Love and Honour* (Jean Saunders, Grafton) in the twenties. Also, in many ways, it's easier to research the near-past, because it's so accessible through books, films, and television series such as *The House of Elliott* and, before that, the theatrical series *The Bretts*. The ensuing book of any similar TV series is always useful for reference.

A detailed book such as *Ragtime to Wartime: The Best of Good Housekeeping 1922–1939* is another great research source. The style of dressing in the twenties has always appealed to me, and there is no lack of information available on fabrics and styles. But the trouble with going into too much detailed research is obviously the time involved, when perhaps one suitable picture will provide you with all the information you need.

Many people will have family photographs relating to earlier years. My mother's wedding photo gave me an instant record of twenties wedding-day attire, with her low-on-the-forehead headdress, short, low-waisted wedding dress and pre-winkle-picker pointed satin shoes. The sepia tint of the photo showed me something about the photography of the time. The detail in your own family records can often surprise you, and save you an enormous amount of time.

The fashions of the twenties are almost legendary now. The low-waisted dresses, the white stockings, the buttoned-bar shoes, the bangles and beads and feathers . . . but what of the prices? Would your housemaid character be able to afford just what she wanted to go 'up west' for a night on the town?

One of the 'Nostalgia' series of books, *Spotlight on the Twenties* by Michael Anglo, gave me many answers. I bought it in a second-hand bookshop in Hay-on-Wye for £4.50, and consider it money well spent, as it has served me for more than one novel. As a dipping-into book, it's a delight to read. For the researcher, it's far more than that. Did you know, for instance, that cami-knickers were very trendy in 1927? And that you could buy a full-length, belted leather coat in Debenhams' sale for under £6? And this was the real thing, remember, no plastic imitations.

The advertising illustrations of Marshall & Snelgrove's winter sale, alongside that of Debenham & Freebody's sale, gave me this, and other, instant sketches of women's fashions, together with the prices. An evening gown for ten and a half guineas . . .? A pure silk Milanese nightgown for thirty-nine and sixpence? A georgette and lace dress and jacket ensemble, listed as a costume at Debenham's, for eight and a half guineas? Probably many of today's younger readers wouldn't even know what those amounts of money meant, but they still conjure up an accurate picture of times past. Those were the days!

One of my 'finds' at a library sale was a marvellous book I bought for 30 pence, called *Cassell's Book of Etiquette* and written by the deliciously mysteriously named author 'A Woman of the World'. (Who was she, I wonder . . .? And why did she go under such an odd pseudonym? Could this even be a starting point for a mystery novel . . .?)

The book was published in 1921, and is an absolute mine of information on the etiquette of the time, together with fascinating pointers into the way people lived, played and behaved in public and private. If you can find it, I thoroughly recommend it for its historical record and little details.

A complete chapter in the book deals with dress, including the style of dress appropriate for different occasions, when paying visits, at garden parties, morning dress, dinner and ball dresses, mourning dress, man's dress, 'full dress', the hat and gloves. One gem of a paragraph compares the Englishwoman of the time rather unfavourably with her French counterpart. We're told that the Parisienne is far more fastidious in such details as her veil, her gloves and her shoes . . .

Materials in use at the time are mentioned. Silks, satins, chiffons and crêpe de Chine, richly trimmed, were the most frequently used fabrics, often worn with a lace mantle or scarf. The toque was becoming very fashionable, and wedding millinery was trimmed with feathers and flowers. Tight lacing and corsets were temporarily out. The sleek boyish line was in.

Sports attire required some amazing detail in the chapter on dress. Skirts, for whatever sport, had to be well above the ankle - five or six inches was not too much! Full-sleeved blouses were in order for tennis, to allow for ample arm movement. Golfing ladies needed a heavy skirt, and if a coat was worn, it should be loose, with no flying ribbons, and for some reason, no jewellery. If the coat needed to be fastened at the neck, then only a good safety-pin brooch was advised.

The golfing garb of the gentlemen described in this most interesting reference book on etiquette reminds me more of Wooster and Jeeves than anything else. So the television version also is not to be overlooked when researching such details visually. But since 'A Woman of the World' presumably wrote a true and faithful record of the times, we must deduce that the knickerbockers and garish hose worn by male golfers were 'the thing'. (I'd like to see my son-in-law in them!)

* * *

37

In the main, the restrictions and conformity of social occasions in times past make surprising reading to those of us who are used to far more informal living. It all makes good copy for the novelist writing about such times, whose characters can duly conform, or be shockingly 'different'.

The basic rules of each decade alone should give the imaginative novelist scope for creating interesting characters and backgrounds. For instance, the young lady coming out at her first ball invariably wore white. But what if your character did not? I leave the rest to you.

A most useful reference book is *The Model Wife, 19th-century style* by Rona Randall, published by the Herbert Press Ltd. In it, she includes vastly detailed information about fashion, underwear, care of clothes, hats, gloves, bags and jewellery. There are many interesting details in the chapter on the care of clothes, not only in the laborious methods used, which are mostly forgotten nowadays with the ease of washing powders and automatic washing machines, but also the dangers the housemaids and others faced when using readily bought household poisons for cleaning or brightening clothes. The possibilities for accident and murder in these innocent procedures soon became obvious, and the fact that gin was used as a cleaning fluid could bring other interesting and boisterous scenes to mind.

If you can track it down in a second-hand bookshop, *Spon's Household Manual*, published in 1887, will tell you a vast amount about middle-class Victorians.

Cosmetics and jewellery

In one form or another, cosmetics have been with us from earliest times. But when did the beauty-spot rage begin and end?

How far back in history has kohl been the most dramatic form of eye make-up? When did rouge cease to be so fashionable? I don't profess to be *au fait* with the answers to these questions - but with a little thought I might find a man who does ...

If I really wanted to get to the heart of a cosmetic industry for my novel I would write to one of the big cosmetic houses and ask them for any information they could give me on the history and workings of their business. If possible I would request a visit to their premises to observe and take notes. (It may not always be possible - such competitive businesses can be very secretive - but it's always worth a try.)

I would also read one of the many books on the subject, such as *The Skin Game* by Gerald McKnight, Sidgwick & Jackson, which gives an alluring insight into how a new cosmetic is launched, as well as covering the eerie fascinations of cosmetic surgery.

As far as cosmetic surgery is concerned, there are frequent horror stories in newspapers about such procedures and results, especially in American tabloids - it would be worth keeping a cuttings file if you should need the information. If you have any American correspondents, enlisting their help in collecting such material would almost certainly be successful. There must be a good side to such surgery too, and a reputable firm would always be glad to set the record straight. Yellow Pages - or your own GP - might provide the name you require.

People have always adorned themselves with jewellery, from Stone Age bone necklaces to precious stones, the favourite Victorian jet jewellery and the craze for gold and glitter. The good old gentleman's pocket watch and chain met its demise in the early part of this century, and what a come-down with the appearance of the far less distinctive digital wrist-watches, plastic et al ... There is plenty of reading matter on jewellery and precious stones in any library.

A small paperback book called *Victoriana* gives illustrated detail of Victorian jewellery, and has provided me with useful and original ideas on adorning my historical heroines. Victorians, in particular, were great innovators of jewellery fashions, as well as everything else.

Children's toys

Nothing pinpoints an era more precisely than the toys with which children surround themselves. When was the hula-hoop so vastly popular? Can you still remember it? They came and went, along with spinning tops and yo-yos and diabolos ... and when did those beautiful china-faced dolls cease to be made, to be replaced by plastic, in more senses than one?

In the series of tiny Bygones Books by Cynthia Roth, published by Corgi, is a book called *Games and Toys of Long Ago*, which gives an excellent run-down of popular toys and the dates in which they were in common use. Toys may not figure very much in your novel, but conversely, an innocent-looking toy could be the lethal weapon with which a crime was committed.

Contemporary details can be found in any catalogue of noted toy manufacturers. For more detailed historical data there are many museums around the country, details of which are given below. All of them are a joy to visit, and guaranteed to take us back to our childhood for a few delightful hours.

But, pleasure apart, in the London Toy and Model Museum you will find a huge collection of model soldiers, dressed in authentic uniforms from the nineteenth century. You can instantly 'see' the uniforms in which the soldiers were dressed when Britain fought the Zulus or the Indian Mutineers, and 'see' the sailors in their distinctive straw hats.

In the Mechanical Music and Doll Connection near Chichester, not only can you find many instruments, musical boxes, mechanical pianos, and the like, but also dolls made of china, and wax Victorian dolls (surely a fire risk, crime novelists ...?), as well as dolls made of velvet and felt which came into fashion in the 1920s.

Games and amusements

The way people kept themselves amused over the centuries has a direct relevance on the ingenuity of inventors, and the materials available at the time. Many of the children's toys have been mentioned above. But what of adults? Allowing your nineteenth-century character to play Trivial Pursuits would obviously be wrong. The game of tennis would seem to be a nineteenth-century invention, yet Henry VIII was known to have played a form of it, and tennis was mentioned in Shakespeare's *Henry V.*

In a historical novel, it's important to keep the flavour of the period in mind, and sometimes what was absolutely accurate still doesn't fit the ambience of the book. If tennis *per se* seems altogether too modern a term for your historical characters, my advice is to let them play something else. This also applies to the language of the period, which will be dealt with in a later chapter.

Some sports, such as shooting, seem to have been with us for ever, but be sure your novel doesn't take place before firearms were invented. A good book on firearms will tell you the dates and details of weapons. Dancing, word games, charades, cards and so on are all amusements that go back to antiquity, as does sitting and talking with friends over food and drink.

The Dunlop Book of Facts lists the origins and antiquity of sport, and we may safely have in any novel characters set before 1850 taking part in any of the following. Some of the activities are quite surprising, since we only think of them in modern terms.

Among these sports are wrestling, falconry, athletics, boxing, fencing, polo, hockey, fly fishing, horse racing, archery, ice skating, bowls, billiards, golf, association football, cricket, fox hunting, caving, bullfighting, rowing, roller skating, baseball, mountaineering, rugby, trotting, swimming, Alpine skiing, ten-pin bowling and rodeo.

After 1850, the range of activities is vastly increased, though actual dates of each sport's origin should be checked. They include the following: gliding, ice hockey, croquet, canoeing, show-jumping, cycling, lawn tennis (as we know it today), snooker, ski jumping, table tennis, netball, motor-cycling, greyhound racing, speedway, sky-diving, aerobatics.

Boswell's *London Journal, 1762–3* provides fine detail of the way eighteenth-century folk of his class spent their leisure time in the coffee houses and in places of more dubious repute. Talking/gossiping with friends would seem to have been a most enjoyable way of passing the time, and one in which perhaps we more privileged folk, with all our electronic gadgets and wizardry, are missing out.

Miscellaneous

How wise or foolish is it to read published novels of the type you wish to write? There are arguments for and against this. There's always the danger of plagiarising other people's works, which no author in his right mind would want to do. But I do think there's a case for immersing yourself in books of a certain type to absorb the flavour of background and setting, and many authors do this.

If you intended to write a novel about the world of horse-racing, for instance, what could be more useful than to read a Dick Francis novel to get the authentic feel of the background? The television series *Trainer* would give you the same sense of a racing stable background. Actually going to a race meeting would certainly give you the atmosphere, the smells, the sense of excitement and the tension. But for any number of personal and economic reasons this is not always feasible, so a vicarious experience, through book or film or magazine, is the obvious answer.

Taking another author's research as gospel can be a tricky thing to do. What if s/he got it wrong? Not only are you compounding the mistake, but making it obvious to anyone with eyes sharp enough to spot it that you merely copied your information. Double-checking from a reliable source must be the rule, so that you don't let your fashionable 1840s lady wear an elaborate hat just because another author included it when the little poke bonnet was suddenly all the rage at that time.

The names you give your characters are important to their times, their occupations and status. A rich source of researching ancient names is the Bible, as are old country churchyards. Cast lists from television programmes and films can provide foreign names, but be sure you know male from female.

Ancient and modern names and their meanings can be found in many books, among them Leslie Dunkling's *Guinness Book of Names*. This aspect of writing is also dealt with in my Allison & Busby book *How to Create Fictional Characters*.

Sources relevant to this chapter

Books (pub. date given where known)

A Concise History of Costume, James Laver, BCA, 1969.

Bygones – Games and Toys of Long Ago, Cynthia Roith, Corgi, 1972.

Cassell's Book of Etiquette, 'A Woman of the World', Cassell, 1921.

Children's Toys Throughout the Ages, Leslie Daiken, Spring Books, 1963.

Costume and Fashion 1760–1920, Jack Cassin Scott, Blandford Press, 1971.

Costume in Context Series (GCSE History List) – *The Regency, The 1940s, The 1950s*, Jennifer Ruby, Batsford, 1963.

Crinolines and Irons: Victorian clothes – how they were cleaned and cared for, Christina Walkley & Vanda Foster, Peter Owen, 1978.

Dressed to Impress 1840–1914, Christina Walkley, Batsford.

English Women's Clothing in the Nineteenth Century, C. W. Cunnington, 1937 (and other books on costume by this author).

Fashion in Costume 1200–1980, Joan Nunn, Herbert Press, 1984.

Fashions in Hair: the first 5000 years, R. Corston, Peter Owen, 1965.

Glass of Fashion, The, Cecil Beaton, Cassell, 1989.

Guinness Book of Names, Leslie Dunkling, Guinness, 1989.

Hand-coloured Fashion-Plates 1770–1899, V. Holland, 1955.

Knickers: An Intimate Appraisal, Rosemary Hawthorne, Souvenir, 1991.

Laundry Bygones, Pamela Sambrook, Shire Publications, 1983.

London Journal, 1762–3, James Boswell, BCA, 1974.

Model Wife, The, 19th century style, Rona Randall, Herbert Press, 1989.

Modes in Hats and Headdresses, R. Turner Wilcox, Scribners, NY, 1959.

New Look, The, Harry Hopkins, Secker & Warburg.

Old Toys, Pauline Flick, Shire Publications, 1985.

People's Chronicle, The, James Trager, Heinemann.

Ragtime to Wartime: The Best of Good Housekeeping 1922– 1939, Ebury Press.

Shops & Shopping, A. Adburgham, Allen & Unwin, 1964.

The Skin Game, Gerald McKnight, Sidgwick & Jackson, 1989.

Spon's Household Manual, E. & F. Spon, 1887.

Spotlight on the Twenties, Michael Anglo, Universal Books, 1985.

Victorian Fashion and Costumes from Harper's Bazaar: 1867– 1898 ed. Stella Blum, Dover, 1974.

Victorian Jewellery, Margaret Flower, Cassell, 1951.

Victoriana, Juri Gabriel, Hamlyn, 1972.

Yesterday's Shopping, David & Charles, Newton Abbot, 1969.

Places to visit

Bethnal Green Museum of Childhood, Cambridge Heath Road, London E2.

Chester Toy Museum, Chester, Cheshire.

Holbache Museum of Childhood, Upper Brook Street, Oswestry, Shropshire.

London Toy and Model Museum, 21–23 Craven Hill, London W2.

Kensington Palace, Kensington Gardens, London W8.

Museum of Costume and Fashion Research Centre (Keeper of Costumes), Assembly Rooms, 4 The Circus, Bath, Avon BA1 2EW.

Museum of Dolls and Bygone Childhood, On A1, nr Newark, Nottinghamshire.

The Queen Elizabeth Gallery of Costume, The Bowes Museum, Barnard Castle, Yorkshire.

York Museum.

Other

Sources mentioned in other chapters will also apply, such as:

TV series, film, video or book, such as *The House of Elliott* and *The Bretts*.

Old magazines and newspapers.

4

HOMES AND FURNISHINGS

How and where did they live?

The characters in a novel can't live in a vacuum. Whether they live in a hovel or a stately home, a 1940s prefab or a space station, at some point it will be necessary for an author to describe that dwelling. In a gothic novel, especially, the gloomy castle or crumbling mansion will have a profound effect on the tense atmosphere the author is trying to create.

Keep in mind also that the homes in which we live are to a considerable degree an extension of our personalities, and that this maxim should be applied to the homes of your fictional people.

The fascination of the TV programme *Through the Keyhole* is a good example of this. We are either amazed or pleased by the intimate look into someone else's life, whether it's by their satisfying clutter or extreme neatness, their colour schemes, their collections, or their taste in music or books that fascinates you. Such authentic detail in your novel will flesh it out, and bring the characters more vividly to life.

I used this in a particular way in one of my own books, *Enchanted Island* by Jean Innes (Silhouette Books USA; F. A. Thorpe, large print; and a *Good Housekeeping* condensed book in America, Spain and Australia). My heroine was an interior designer with the unique approach of suggesting colour schemes and furnishings for her clients by using their astrological traits.

In this book, the house itself . . . well, I could say that it didn't need much more than imagination to describe it. And yet, I have never lived in such a house, so I was obviously drawing on what I had seen, whether in a modest mansion open to the public, or from a scene from a TV programme which could have given me the basics. You don't *always* need to travel far and wide to get what you need. Your own town, if not your armchair viewing or reading, may well provide the answer.

Since the house in my novel was Victorian-built, I got most of the architectural and interior details from *The World of Victoriana* by James Norbury, Hamlyn, right here on my bookshelf. The house in my book is situated in Jersey. Thus –

. . . it was like a grey sentinel, so ugly and yet so quaintly beautiful, with both English and French influences on the architecture. The tall grey turrets with a pearly sheen on them in the sunlight were reminiscent of French chateaux; the solidly built stone frontage with rows and rows of mullioned windows was like an English country mansion;

And later –

The high ceilings with their ornate cornices and centre roses were dingy and cracked in places. The walls of the entrance hall and the drawing room into which Shelley was shown were of dark brown wood panels, the carpets faded floral. Much of the furniture was extremely good at first glance, and highly polished, but the whole place was so cluttered it didn't do justice to the fine pieces.

Since one of my aims in *How To Research Your Novel* is to allay the dread of 'having to do all that research', I include these brief excerpts to show how little actual research was needed in this case to create an immediate atmosphere. Such exterior descriptions would be shown in any travel brochure of English and French hotels. The ceiling description came directly from a rather decrepit flat my son once occupied. Dark panelling was an obvious choice to present the gloom of the place before the heroine got to work on it.

The rest of it was hardly a problem for any creative author to describe. Don't be so bogged down by the thought of seeking out accurate references that you can't also use your own experience and imagination, and the simple sources in your own magazine rack. Any good magazine of the *Homes and Gardens* variety will show you plenty of interior decors to describe or adapt.

Depending on your book, there is a bewildering variety of styles of architecture, buildings and interiors in which to house your characters and bring them to life for your readers. How detailed or how briefly you describe these dwellings depends on you and your book, but I believe it greatly enhances the believability in your characters to set them down in a residence in which they – and you – will be comfortable.

Gardens

Gardens have always played a big part in home ownership, from the magnificent ornate gardens of Versailles to the humble cottage garden so beloved by our nineteenth-century forebears. Describing a garden in a novel is mostly a matter for the imagination and preference – providing you don't have summer roses flowering in December, or daffodils in August, or fill your fictional historical garden with plants that hadn't yet arrived in Britain at that time. And don't stock your breezy outdoor gardens with plants that won't flourish without the benefit of a tropical or hothouse atmosphere.

However easy it may seem to mention the contents of a garden, whether it contains flowers or herbs or vegetables, it pays to check on the season, the availability and the location. What flourishes in profusion in the sheltered areas of Cornwall will probably stand no chance in the wilds of northern Scotland. In many cases, it's simple enough to observe what's growing in your own garden at any given season, or to check on the seed packets at any garden centre for blooming times, as well as inspiration.

The books of Dr D. G. Hessayon that cover specific aspects of plants, trees and so on, can be found in many homes. But one of the most useful and fascinating for the researcher into gardens, whether small or magnificent, is a more comprehensive book called *The Armchair Book of the Garden*. If you wanted to describe a beautiful formal garden without leaving your own living-room, then any of the beautiful illustrations in this book, together with background detail about the people who created them, will tell you all you needed to know. This is not just another gardening book. There is also the history of the garden as we know it, and an illustrated glossary of old gardening tools. Some of them were quite lethal-looking, and would make excellent murder weapons . . .

There is also practical information. How to grow your own cake decorations . . . how to make a terrarium . . . how to make flower perfume . . . how to make flower cosmetics. There are the names and explanations of many items that go to make up the formal garden, such as the ice-house and the ha-ha, the folly and the parterre.

An extra bonus is the section on being your own garden lawyer. For instance, what do you do if someone is hurt in your garden? You can find out on page 215 of this absorbing book.

From paupers to royalty

If you're writing a book about down-and-outs, there's obviously no research needed to describe a cardboard box, a narrow alleyway or city doorway. Fortunately, the majority of us don't have to endure such privations, and live in ordinary, modest houses, flats, farmhouses or mansions, according to our background, status and inclinations.

Some of the theme parks already mentioned, such as Flambards in Cornwall, and Morwellham Quay in Devon, show the interiors of wartime homes and workers' cottages respectively. The York Museum also authentically reconstructs a Victorian street, as does the Beamish complex in Northumberland. Such careful reconstructions will show you the interiors of the cottages as they were then, and most of these places have illustrated booklets that you can buy quite cheaply rather than relying on your memory of the rooms when you return home.

But a walk through any small rural village, armed with a camera, can give you a true record of the exterior construction of thatched cottages and stone-built houses, many of which have the building dates inscribed on the stonework. I have done this many times in Dorset and Cornwall and other places. In Norfolk, as well as showing the exterior views, the Trinity Hospital Almshouses are open for public viewing.

Historic Farm Buildings by Jeremy Lake (Blandford Press), gives a detailed study of agricultural buildings and their uses. Farming museums, such as Rydale Folk Museum, Hutton-le-Hole, North Yorkshire, will also show you the general detail of barns, outhouses and integral occupations within the farming scene. There are many places like this in rural areas, and a reference work such as the AA's *Places to Visit in Britain*, published by Hodder & Stoughton, lists many.

One working farm-cum-museum that I found especially useful was Sheppy's Cider near Taunton. The collection of cider-making equipment was of special interest for my Rowena Summers novel *The Sweet Red Earth* (Severn House/Sphere), which is set in the apple-growing and cider-making industries of the area. Taunton is within easy reach of my home, and in one visit I was able to glean an amazing amount of information to incorporate in my novel. I could actually see the nineteenth-century cider press and equipment, and find out how they worked from the various leaflets in the museum. Such visual detail enhanced the reading I had already done on the subject.

An added bonus to the visit was a television programme in which the director wanted to film a small scene from one of my books. They chose a scene from *The Sweet Red Earth*, with myself reading as voiceover, and this was filmed in the cider-press museum section of Sheppy's Cider. Together with a brief look at my working life at home, and a trip to a local bookshop with my books carefully arranged, it took all day to film and ended up as about three minutes on the screen. That's television. But it was certainly worth the experience of seeing how the director and camera crew worked, if I ever want to write a chapter in a novel about an author having a scene from a book filmed. Nothing should be wasted in the cause of research. And yes, I took notes.

Stately and less-than-stately homes

If you're a member of the National Trust, then its annual Handbook will give you all the information you need on their houses and other properties open to visitors. As a member, you will know that entry to many of these properties is free, or offered at reduced entry fees than to the general public.

A visit or telephone call to the information bureau of any large town will also tell you of such places in the vicinity.

There's no easier way to see the trappings and ornate lifestyles of times past than visiting stately homes, of which there is such an abundance in Britain.

If you're particularly interested in period design and furnishings, then an excellent reference work is Judith and Martin Miller's *Period Style*. Not only does this book have around 700 colour photographs, but it also has a detailed directory listing museums to visit, together with details of courses on period architecture and interiors.

I'm not suggesting it would ever be necessary to go to such extremes of research for what after all, might constitute only a small part of a novel. But if you really want to immerse yourself in the kind of house your characters would occupy, and you can spare the time, it may well be worth while. Certainly, if you had never been inside a nunnery before, for example, and needed to evoke such an atmosphere, then such a visit would probably be essential.

A TV playwright once described in an interview how he went into a psychiatric ward for two weeks to absorb the atmosphere for a play, and, rather chillingly, described how, when he had donned the cardigan-and-slippers uniform of the inmates, he was so readily accepted as one of them. Other writers will enter hospital wards and follow discreetly as the staff go about their business. In a book or play with such a background, a hospital becomes a second home to the characters, and needs to be described just as accurately.

It would be stretching credulity to consider a police station a house or home, except perhaps to the people who work there and spend endless hours there, day and night. So this is my excuse for including a small anecdote about an English writer on holiday in New York. Seeing a battered police car parked outside a police precinct, she was keen to take a photograph for reference for her novel.

Wisely, she obtained permission, and was then invited into

the precinct where she was given coffee, shown the cells and the book of 'mug-shots', had the entire workings of the daily routine explained to her without even asking, and witnessed the arrival and booking of two suspects. The precinct was certainly 'home' for its officers, and my friend vouchsafed for the authenticity of such American TV shows as *Hill Street Blues* and *Cagney and Lacey*.

Quite often, simply the flavour of a house or building is all that it is required to evoke the feeling of 'being there', which is essentially what a novelist aims to achieve.

There are vast numbers of books available on homes and housing in any library or bookshop. Every town will have local-interest books, showing the town's development. I have a collection of books on Bristol, especially those detailing the changes during and since the Second World War. *Bristol as It Was, 1939–1914* by Reece Winstone is just one of the late author's wonderful books recording his home city, using many photographs to illustrate buildings and streets.

As far as real stately homes are concerned, to describe one of them in a novel should present no problem. Open to the public are such wonderful edifices as Castle Howard in Yorkshire, Chatsworth in Derbyshire, Windsor Castle, Althorp House, Osborne House on the Isle of Wight, the Royal Pavilion, Brighton, with its Regency exhibition, Queen Mary's House in Jedburgh, or Anne of Cleve's House, Lewes.

Clevedon Court is only a short distance away from my home, as is the Georgian House in Bristol, and almost everyone will have something of similar interest near where they live. The brief list above is only a fraction of the many accessible places countrywide from which an exploration can give colour and realism to your historical novels. Others are listed at the end of this chapter, but these can only give a brief idea of the hundreds of properties open to the public.

The new writer may automatically think that such great houses belong only in a historical novel, but if so, he is not looking beyond the obvious. Stately homes can be put to admirable use in contemporary novels. Since these once-remote houses have become tourist attractions, they have to be staffed in all kinds of capacities by people like us, who don't wear crinolines or have the restrictions of our Victorian counterparts.

All kinds of people, from tour guides to cleaners and gardeners, safari park staff, gift-shop assistants, and restaurant staff and chefs, make up the teams that now serve the stately homes open to the public. So why not a murder story set in a stately home? Or a crime of major proportions? Or a science-fiction novel, or children's novel? Supposing one of the little darlings decided to linger behind on a school trip, and found himself involved in some kind of time-warp . . .? The possibilities are endless.

I have visited Longleat House in Wiltshire many times, but never so absorbingly as on the occasion I went there with an invited group of American romance authors. We not only took afternoon tea with the late Lord and Lady Bath, but were shown the priceless collection of books in the private wing of the house by Lord Bath's son, Lord Christopher Thynne.

Because this was an organised group visit, we were taken into rooms where the ordinary paying punter is not allowed. We saw the vast collection of Winston Churchill memorabilia, and the Adolf Hitler collection, and even later, we were taken up on the roof.

You may think that this was a strange place to visit. But not if you saw the beautiful countryside panorama surrounding the estate that the normal visitor never sees, and not if you heard, as we did, how, in times past, the family used to hold teas and even dances up there on that splendid and enormous area of flat roof. One wondered if they still do . . .

Listening to such fascinating details of a way of life few of us could ever imagine, it was almost possible to 'hear' the tinny sounds of the gramophone, and 'see' the floaty chiffon dresses of the 1920s flappers swaying in the arms of their eager young gentlemen. And to imagine the organisation, the teams of maids and servants, laboriously carrying everything on to the roof, and the sight of the formal, damask-spread tables, the food and the wine . . . And I'm sure that more than one of those romantic authors was already weaving a story around such an occasion. It was a heady day, and gave a magical glimpse into another lifestyle.

Lighting and heating

The practical novelist will begin to wonder how these vast buildings could ever be adequately lit and heated. These are only a few of the things that have changed greatly over the centuries. When we write our novels, we need to be sure which form of lighting to let our people use, though in many cases it will be quite obvious. Obviously, cavemen never knew the simple luxury of electric lighting. But we can go from firelight to candlelight; from oil lamps to flares to gas-light; from electric lighting to solar lighting. And in all these cases we need to know in which period such lights were in favour.

It would be quite wrong to have a nineteenth-century heroine visiting a theatre with flickering gas-lights, for instance, before such things were in popular use. And it's perilously easy to slip up. I know. On this very fact, I was queried by my editor, and it had been a grey area in my researches. Fortunately, this was well before publication, and it was an easy thing to get around. I couldn't readily find out when gas lighting was common in theatres, but I got around it by merely leaving out any mention of lighting altogether. There are always ways . . .

No matter how colourful the imagery of a scene that you bring to your novel, twisting history to suit your plot is most definitely to be avoided. But so is spending a ridiculous amount of time on a research fact that can just as easily be left out. Ask yourself if it's really necessary to include the information, and then act accordingly.

An excellent little book in my collection is called *Lamps and Lighting* in the Bygones series of Corgi mini-books. Alas, these tiny volumes must surely be long out of print, but will give you an idea of the kind of book to look out for. When I bought it, some years ago, it cost me twenty pence, and is filled with a wealth of information.

The book, researched and written by Cynthia Roith, details such fascinating objects as candle-snuffers, candle-moulds and candle-boxes, and accessories such as tinder boxes, tinder pistols and horns, fire-steels, matches and lighters. An entire past era is practically conjured up by the contents page alone. The book is also illustrated, and many of the photos are acknowledged to be from the Science Museum in London. It is intended to be a collector's handbook, but is also of immense use to the historical researcher, costing just pence and taking up little room on a shelf. Because of the costs that *can* be involved in doing research, I repeat what I said in my introduction: it need not necessarily cost a fortune to find out the things you need to know to flesh out your novel and give it credulity.

I discovered another snippet of information about lighting in this small book. In the Channel Islands, in the days of oil lamps, where crusies were known as *crassets* or *croissets*, the colour of the light held certain superstitions. If it burned greenish, there were witches about. If it burned blue, it heralded windy conditions. If anyone was touched by flying sparks, there was news on the way, and possibly an invitation.

Such snippets as these are useful to file away, since they can be used exactly as they are in the locations mentioned. Or they can be adapted to whatever time and location suits your story. Who is to say that such a superstition did not exist in your invented town or island or family setting?

Furniture and antiques

A reference book dealing with the methods of repairing, restoring and caring for antiques could be invaluable for the novelist researching such an occupation. Souvenir Press has just the thing in its trade paperback, *Antiques: Professional Secrets for the Amateur*, which lengthy title seems to sum up the contents admirably.

I have two little books on antiques that I have found useful whenever I needed to include items of furniture and other knick-knacks in my novels. One is a paperback previously mentioned for its inclusion of Victorian jewellery. Called simply *Victoriana*, by Juri Gabriel, it cost me 60 pence and gives splendid colour illustrations of sofas, chairs, tables, sideboards, desks and many items in the kitchen and the bedroom, as well as silver, pottery, glassware, embroidery, metalwork and much more. In every way, it's a little gem of a book.

It has been suggested that more items of furniture were produced during Queen Victoria's reign than in the previous centuries put together, so it's no wonder that much of the antique furniture we see today is of nineteenth-century origin. This makes a visit to a house auction or general auction of particular interest to the historical novelist, as does the fascination of the television programme *The Antiques Road Show*.

My second small book is a hardback that cost me ten pence second hand. It's called simply *Collecting English Antiques* by

Arthur Harding, and covers similar topics to the other, but over a wider time span. Among other details, it lists the dates when Minton, Coalport, Spode and Wedgewood pottery and porcelain were first produced, their distinctive markings, and how to recognise fakes. As with most reference books, there are useful bibliographies for further reading.

Sources relevant to this chapter

Books

Antiques: Professional Secrets for the Amateur, Michael Doussy, Souvenir Press, 1989.

Armchair Book of the Garden, The, Dr D. G. Hessayon, PBI Publications, 1986.

Art Nouveau, Mario Amaya, Studio Vista, London, 1966.

Bristol as It Was 1939–1914, Reece Winstone, publisher, 1978.

Bygones: Lamps and Lighting, Cynthia Roith, Corgi minibooks, 1972.

Collecting English Antiques, Arthur Harding, Foyles Handbooks, 1963.

Historic Farm Buildings, Jeremy Lake, Blandford Press, 1989.

Nineteenth-Century British Glass, Hugh Wakefield, Faber, 1961.

Nineteenth-Century English Furniture, E. Aslin, Faber, 1962.

Period Style, Judith & Martin Miller, Mitchell Beazley, 1989.

Places to Visit in Britain, AA Hodder & Stoughton, 1988.

Victoriana, Juri Gabriel, Hamlyn, 1972.

Victorian Silver and Silver-plate, Patricia Wardle, Herbert Jenkins, 1963.

World of Victoriana, The, James Norbury, Hamlyn, 1972.

Places to visit

Althorp House, nr Northampton, Northants.
Anne of Cleves' House, Southover, Lewes, East Sussex.
Badminton House, Great Badminton, Gloucestershire.
Blenheim Palace, Woodstock, Oxon.
Castle Howard, fifteen miles NE of York, N. Yorkshire.
Chatsworth House, nr Matlock, Derbyshire.
Clevedon Court, Clevedon, nr Bristol, Avon.
The Georgian House, Bristol.
Hever Castle, Hever, nr Edenbridge, Kent.
Longleat House, nr Warminster, Wiltshire.
Osborne House, nr East Cowes, Isle of Wight.
Sheppy's Cider, nr Taunton, Somerset.
Petworth House, Petworth, Sussex.
Royal Pavilion, Brighton.
Trinity Hospital Almshouses, Castle Rising, Norfolk.
Warwick Castle, Warwick.
Windsor Castle, Windsor.

Other

Hill Street Blues, TV series.
Cagney and Lacey, TV series.
Antiques Road Show, TV series.
Homes and Gardens magazine, and others.

Sources mentioned in other chapters will also apply.

5

THE LIVES OF ORDINARY PEOPLE

Class systems

Exploiting age-old class systems is one of the most useful assets for a novelist. Various examples: pitting the workers against the bosses, as in the Peter Sellers film *I'm All Right Jack*; the pretty little housemaid seduced by the lordly son of the house, as in Barbara Taylor Bradford's *A Woman of Substance*; the struggle for survival between the poor, intelligent boy and the rich man's son; the power struggle between different races, when one of them thinks it superior to the other; school bullying; and snobbery.

The list is endless, and however much we may despise some or all of it, it provides a rich source of material for the novelist. Nor can we pretend that class strata don't exist. They always have, and always will. The monarchy alone is evidence of the divisions between 'them' and 'us'. Because of their 'accessibility' in modern times, with their performances on television, and public appearances, we think we know the Royals, but we don't. Their world is completely different from that of the majority of us, and few would wish to live in their goldfish bowl.

But there is still a definite pecking order among us more ordinary mortals. From the army general to the sergeant-major to the private, we live in our allotted layers of society. From the princess to the housemaid, we all know our place. All these varying layers of human life, and people's reactions to each other, are a godsend to the novelist, but don't forget that it's often when the novelist takes a character *out* of his or her allotted place that the fun, and the story, begins.

Many a novel has begun with this premise. The 'fish out of water' syndrome is often a good starting point to bring out all the hidden resentment and belligerence of a character, for instance. This might be an appropriate point to mention a book called *Crises*, subtitled *A Guide to your Emotions*. Written by agony aunt Irma Kurtz, it gives a detailed insight into human relationships, and in particular, to the huge variety of emotional crises and stresses that people can put each other through. I doubt that the book was written as a research manual, but it can be quite useful in thinking up new and less predictable ways to develop your characters' emotional turmoils.

Any magazine with an agony column in it will give you brief insights into problems and answers on similar and other themes, though not in so much depth. But if just the answers you need for your characters' problems are there, and all for the price of a magazine, why not use them?

Starting your own cuttings file of such agony columns is worth a thought. But I advise you to sub-divide your file into the problems they contain, such as sexual, marital, new mothers, childhood illnesses, house problems, gardening problems, DIY difficulties, legal matters and so on, or you'll end having to wade through the whole lot in order to find that snippet you vaguely remember putting away somewhere . . .

I've been a collector of old postcards for some time now, and have always filed my postcards, covering the last hundred years or so, in sections relating to travel, royalty, political events, leisure activities, inventions and so on. It was some while before I realised I was doing this all wrong. What I needed was to have a comprehensive view of a period, so that I had an all-round view of events that happened in any given time, such as the 1920s or 1930s, for example. Once I rearranged my filing system into decades, it was much easier to 'see' a period and all the social events, dramas and changing lifestyles that were most important to it.

Conventions

The conventions of everyday life range from how a baby is trained to walk and talk in the manner of his parents, to wedding-day rituals and funeral arrangements. In other words, from birth to death we're constricted in many ways by the etiquette of the day, and none of us can escape it. Whether or not we choose to live by the conventions of the day is another matter, and is why the rebels are often so much more interesting to write about than the holier-than-thous! But to know how such characters would rebel, you need to know what the rules are in the first place. Social convention is relatively easy to research or absorb, but what of the conventions pertaining to activities?

I once wanted to write about a teenage rebel in one of my teenage novels, *Anchor Man* (Jean Saunders, William Heinemann), which was going to be set entirely in a pot-hole underneath the Mendip Hills in Somerset. Firstly, I read up everything I could on the right way to go about caving. This included the recommendations about sensible clothing, the proper lighting equipment, ropes, food supplies and so on. Having researched all the right way to go about pot-holing, I made my reckless characters do exactly the opposite, putting themselves in great danger, and thus creating an exciting plot.

The accepted etiquette of our lives changes more swiftly than we think. The 'permissive society' was an outrage in its heyday, but the term itself has almost passed into nostalgia now, along with winklepickers, DA haircuts, teddy-boy clothes, and flower-power children. We forget so quickly.

If I were to write a novel with a 1950s background, I would need to research it well – and yet I was there. I was married in the fifties, but since I was occupied with things other than writing novels, I remember little of it in great detail, unless I seriously put my mind to it. A marvellous book I bought at Hay-on-Wye is called *Have You Forgotten Yet?*, subtitled *Between the Two World Wars*. The title is self-explanatory, and both text and illustrations cover a fascinating period in great detail.

There have always been accepted ways of doing things. But they change over the years, and this is something for the novelist to be aware of. Until early in this century, black-edged mourning-cards, which are seldom seen nowadays, certainly in 'ordinary circles', were the order of the day. These were far more than a mere notification of someone's death. I have a personal reason to know this. My paternal grandfather died in 1905, at the early age of 35, and the funeral party was supplied with the expected printed mourning-cards. These contained not only all the details of his death, but also a very poignant and personal poem. Unless anyone can prove otherwise, I have always assumed that my grandmother actually wrote (or adapted) it, and if this is so, then she must have been the original writer in my family. The words are as follows:

> Farewell to thee, my husband dear;
> Sleep on and take your rest.
> I know you really are not here,
> But there among the blest.
>
> I know you will not come again,
> But I will come to thee,
> When time has said the Great Amen,
> And God has called for me.

Meantime, I'll work with heart and hands,
And wait right patiently,
To tend our five dear little ones,
And still remember thee.

Annie Wilkins

Such sentiments sum up the way people spoke and wrote from their hearts in those days, without the sophisticated restrictions we put on ourselves nowadays. I discovered this same frankness and willingness to express the emotions when I researched the First World War for my novel *The Bannister Girls* (Jean Saunders, W. H. Allen/Grafton), details of which will come in the final chapter.

Language and slang

Regional and foreign variations in speech can be readily found nowadays in any radio play, film or television programme, especially the soap operas. We are far more fortunate than writers of an earlier era in that we can have instant access to such things without leaving the comfort of our armchairs.

But when it comes to the actual words your characters use in their dialogue, take heart. Historical novelists generally agree that it's a mistake to overuse dialect in dialogue, and to use too many 'authentic' rural words. If a reader has difficulty reading your carefully researched 'authentic' language, she won't read on, and will simply skip those passages. Make your dialogue natural, with just the flavour of the region or period, and you won't go far wrong.

A favourite source for many historical novelists is the *Penguin Book of Historical Slang*. This can also provide hours of amusement from the sheer naughtiness of some of the phrases our ancestors used to use! The only drawback to this book from a research viewpoint, is that you have to know the word or phrase you want to check in order to see when it first came into popular use. But having said that, you will un-doubtedly discover some ripe new ones in the process.

Television programmes past and present can provide a rich source of language, slang and dialect study. Obvious ones include *Coronation Street, Eastenders, Brookside, Upstairs, Downstairs, You Rang, M'Lord?, Neighbours, 'Allo, 'Allo, Auf Weidersein, Pet, Emmerdale, The Liver Birds, Only Fools and Horses, Take the High Road, Strathblair* and many more. Don't dismiss their value in portraying the way people speak and behave in their local environments and situations.

Australian and American soap operas also provide us with many idioms we probably never knew existed. Before *Neighbours*, for example, did you know what it meant to 'shoot through'? Don't overlook these soap operas, even those you may dislike, as sources for oft-used phrases.

Your research finds can come from unlikely sources. I'm a crossword addict, and when one of my daughters bought me a book called *Crossword Lists*, I discovered it included section-alised lists of words, covering a vast range of subjects. You may not readily think of this book in connection with re-searching your novel, but its usefulness for me has gone far beyond merely looking up a seven- or twelve-letter word to fit a crossword clue. You can find starter information on many subjects, including: wedding anniversaries, peerage, heraldic terms, American Indians, French phrases, stadiums and venues, materials, decorations and medals, religious orders, computer programme language, geological time scale, medical terms, musical terms, world leaders, breeds of dogs/cattle/horses, volcanoes, professions, trades and occupations, architectural terms, trophies, events and awards, weapons, abbreviations. Not bad, for a book that doesn't profess to be a research manual. I stress that the main usefulness of this type of book is for starter information – but you have to start somewhere.

Food and drink

I don't believe in spending an inordinate amount of time researching the kinds of foods and drink in which my characters indulged themselves, but a certain amount of research is necessary. It's too easy to be brought up short when you've set them all down at a medieval banquet, for instance, to realise that you don't have the faintest idea what to serve them, or how many courses they would have.

Most libraries usually have a section on food and drink, or one of the manuals already listed will have a section devoted to it. Rona Randell's *The Model Wife, Nineteenth-Century Style*, for instance, has a chapter entitled 'On Becoming a Good Cook'. Not only does Ms Randell give many fascinating details of food and drink applicable for the time, but also methods of cooking it, and actual recipes.

In 1819 yet another anonymous lady author wrote *A New System of Domestic Cookery* by 'A Lady'. She was subsequently known to be a Mrs M. Rundell ... it's odd to note the similarity of author names, quite unconnected.

If you want to know more about the earlier tools of the cooking trade, then two useful books are *Firegrates and Kitchen Ranges* and *Old Cooking Utensils*, both by David J. Eveleigh, Shire Publications. Alternatively, a day out at one of the great houses, such as Longleat House, with their gleaming kitchens on display, will give you an instant picture of what they were like.

Past great novelists such as Jane Austen, the Brontës, Thomas Hardy, Charles Dickens and so on will easily provide you with the kind of food and drink that was in vogue, since eating and drinking was one of the preoccupations of the time. For modern methods on cooking and wine-making, any good book at any library will give you a substantial background knowledge.

In my own collection I have a book called *Sainsbury's Book of Wine* by Oz Clarke, published for J. Sainsbury by Webster's Wine Guides. If you want to know the story of wine, from growing the grapes and every stage to the final production of the wine, this book is a gem of a manual, and is also well illustrated. It also tells you which wines best complement which foods, and goes into great detail about climate, soil conditions, classifications of wines, taste, vintages et cetera, in a variety of wine-producing countries, including France, Spain, Portugal and the United States. There is an A-Z of wines and wine terms, and if you were to ally such a book with the visual impact of a TV series such as *Falcon Crest*, you would need to look no further for all the authentic detail for a novel's wine-making background.

Food in History and *Sex in History* are two books that give an overall look at the many changing ideas of the times, including the harems in the Middle East, how they developed, and how they worked. And *The Weaker Vessel* looks at the lives of women during the seventeenth century.

Occupations

Magazines and books covering every kind of occupation are freely available, and it would be futile to try and cover a long list of them here. But, just as in the section above, don't ignore the usefulness of television programmes that give you a bird's-eye view of the way people live and behave in work situations. I frequently refer to TV, because anything visual gives you a far more instant idea of other people's lifestyles. Examples are programmes such as *Falcon Crest* for the wine-making industry; *London's Burning* for a marvellous insight into the dangers and traumas that firemen face – and for the kind of necessary relief laughter that's also attributed to hospital sitcoms; *Trainer* for horse-racing and training background; *All Creatures Great and Small* for a vet's life.

There have been so many police programmes over the years, we must surely all know the call signs by now, and also the way police stations are run. For more precise information, your local police station is only a walk, a bus ride, a letter or a phone call away.

Occupations of earlier times can be discovered quite easily through reading. Library shelves are full of such reference books as my copy of *How They Lived, 1700–1815*, bought in a library sale for 50 pence. With first-hand passages by writers of the time, it includes a mass of information on all aspects of life during that time.

The chapter on Work describes work on the land; estate work; expert work; genteel work; housework; women's work; child labour, and others. It includes details of manual work, and prices charged for such work. Some housemaids' instructions are as follows: 'To use as little soap as possible (if any) in scowering rooms. All rooms to be dry-scrubbed with white sand. Never to dust pictures, nor the frames or anything that has a gilt edge. When a floor cloth wants washing, not to use a brush or soapsuds, but a soft linen and some fresh milk and water.' To me, those few sentences sum up the hardship of the poor housemaid more than adequately.

And how about a woman's payment for harvest work in 1787? There was fruit-picking or haymaking at four pence a day, making the grand total of four shillings for two weeks' work! Of course, she could always work in a factory making handkerchiefs for 4/6d a dozen.

How They Lived is one of a series of books of immense usefulness to the researcher, as is the series *They Saw It Happen*, covering various periods in history, from 55 BC, right up until 1940.

One of the cheapest and most useful little reference books I ever bought was another of the school project books called *The Life of the Farm*. It was number 001 in a series simply called A Project Book, covering a variety of topics, and exclusive to Woolworths. The book is packed with information that a novelist would find useful, and includes a bibliography that lists many other books on farming – not bad value for eight pence.

Autobiographies and memoirs about life in various parts of the country can yield a rich source of material for the novelist. *Countryman on the Broads* (bought in a library sale for 35 pence), was written by a man who recalled his boyhood there in fascinating detail. As the blurb says, 'Oliver Ready gave us his private world', and I learned more about the general working life, the flora, seasons, pastimes and dialect of East Anglia from this volume than from any textbook or my several holidays on the Norfolk Broads. I incorporated much of this insight into my novel *The Savage Moon* (Rowena Summers, Severn House/Sphere).

One writer, setting her novel in the magazine fiction world, wrote to one of the popular teenage magazines requesting permission to be unpaid dogsbody for a week, to observe how things worked. She stated her reasons for her 'work in progress'. There were no objections, and the writer found it invaluable as authentic background detail and atmosphere for her novel. It's not only the obvious places, such as factories and craft workshops that can provide help.

The National Trust Book of *Forgotten Household Crafts* takes you behind the scenes to the implements and lifestyles of our grandparents and great-grandparents. Here you will find fascinating details of such forgotten artefacts as the wash boiler, the dangle-spit, a varied collection of tools for chopping, pounding and pulping in the kitchen, and much more. Among the subjects covered are salting and pickling, making and using cream, making lye and soap, dyeing, lace-making, keeping bees, stencilling, ornamenting the home, et cetera. You can find so much information in a highly illustrated volume, such as this one. I call it a pot-pourri of a book, and it contains all an author would need to flavour an historical novel with kitchen methods and husbandry occupations.

Many National Trust properties have examples of the way our hard-working forefathers had to work without the aid of modern machinery, from Victorian kitchen displays to dairies, butteries and the like. Some other kitchens worth visiting are to be found at Landhydrock in Cornwall. Examples of early bathrooms can be seen at Castle Drogo in Devon, and at Kedleston Hall in Derbyshire. In Uppark, near Petersfield, West Sussex, you can see a butler's pantry, laid out with all the intricacies of the cleaning materials required in far-off days.

It is possible to name only a tiny fraction of the properties open to the public, where research is a pleasure as well as an eye-opener to the ways our ancestors used their ingenuity, skill and sheer elbow-grease to live their lives. Some of these have already been mentioned, where you can see people dressed in authentic costume demonstrating the old crafts.

Potteries, such as Brannan's Pottery in Barnstaple, Devon, give guided tours, with supervised throwing of its terracotta pottery, and this one also has a museum giving the historical background of the industry. Dartington Crystal in Devon is where fine crystal is blown and crafted. This also has factory tours, and an exhibition showing the production and history of glass.

In Wendron, Cornwall, the Poldark Mine and Heritage Complex has a cinema showing the history of Cornish tin, together with an exhibition of eighteenth- and nineteenth-century exhibits and restored mining cottages. There is also the eight-eenth-century 'underground experience' of a Cornish tin mine.

For contemporary occupations, my library has a huge book simply titled *Occupations*. This details over 600 jobs and careers of all types. It includes the type of work involved in each job, working conditions, pay and prospects, training, and related occupations. This can be very useful when you're deciding what job to give your characters.

Medicines, nursing and childbirth

Most novels eventually see one or more of the characters ending up with medical problems. (Test it and see.) Hospital procedures obviously need a great degree of accuracy. *The Lancet* has long been one of the prime medical journals, and there are others of equal use for reference. Nor is it only writers of doctor–nurse romances who need to describe illnesses or accidents in their novels, especially those taking place in wartime. I have had various characters as doctors and nurses, in and out of hospitals, in my novels. And while I would advise any author to go to expert sources for details of the oldest or the latest techniques in surgery and other treatment, we probably all have items in our own homes for simpler researches. Personally, I'm not addicted to buying medical books - although I'm not a hypochondriac, I could easily think myself into every obscure disease. But glancing through my own book shelves at random, I could refer to some excellent books such as *First Aid*, the excellent and authorised manual of the St John Ambulance Association and Brigade (maybe I'd be too squeamish to follow the procedures for emergency childbirth - but I could certainly direct a character in a novel into the right procedures).

My edition of *Pears Cyclopaedia* is dated, but has a whole

section on medical matters, diseases and remedies. Some time ago I saved the six free sections of *The Encyclopedia of Health* (The A–Z of Common Complaints and Cures) published in association with *Today* newspaper, more in the interests of research than in discovering what symptoms I might or might not have.

There are always weekly or monthly women's magazines in the house, and they invariably contain health pages. Anything of possible use I cut out and keep in a cuttings file labelled 'Medical'. I list the title of each new cutting on a cover sheet inside the clear plastic cover. It's a very simple method, but has proved more than adequate for my research needs.

Most of us have such sources right under our noses, and probably never think about them when we want to give our characters some interesting complaint, or wonder what to do about a fictional broken ankle until the ambulance arrives.

And never forget personal experience. On holiday in Florida I severely injured my back, and spent the next nine days receiving treatment from a chiropractor. This was a new (and very unwelcome) experience, but despite the considerable pain from the injury, I wrote up all the daily procedures, with a few relevant photographs taken by my husband, and the wasted part of a holiday may yet emerge in a novel.

Visits to museums showing old surgical instruments will add to the horror of medicine – and dentistry – in times past. The German underground hospitals in Jersey and Guernsey are grim reminders of operating theatres of the not-so-distant past. A hundred years ago surgery was performed without the benefit of anaesthetics, and the suffering it entailed can only be imagined. The Wellcome Historical Medical Museum in London is also well worth a visit. Those rip-roaring scenes in Hollywood movies of cowboy heroes being given swigs of whisky to dull their senses before their bullets were removed were not so far-fetched after all.

The Faber Book of Reportage is for strong stomachs; there

is an account of Fanny Burney's unanaesthetised mastectomy in 1811, for example. There are many such vivid accounts of past horrors, many of them told by eye-witnesses.

Forensic Medicine by Professor Alan Watson could be useful for crime novelists, *Gray's Anatomy* for the science-fiction writer and others. *Black's Medical Dictionary* gives an overall view of the subject, and there are any number of specialist reference works that a library could obtain for you. Enlist the help of your friendly librarian and involve him in your project.

Any of your family's hospital experiences can prove useful, and it's worth keeping a diary of your own stay in hospital. *Anatomy of a Hospital* gives an insight into the daily running of a hospital from the staff viewpoint. Finally, don't forget the many leaflets in doctors' waiting-rooms that may give you the basic information you need, or start you off on further research with addresses to contact.

Sources relevant to this chapter

Books (pub. dates given where known)

Anatomy of a Hospital, Julian Ashley, OUP.
Black's Medical Dictionary, William A. R. Thomson, Black, 1984.
Countryman on the Broads, Oliver G. Ready, Macgibbon & Kee, 1910 and 1967.
Crises, A Guide to Your Emotions, Irma Kurtz, Ebury Press, 1981.
Crossword Lists, Anne Stibbs, Bloomsbury, 1989.
Faber Book of Reportage, The, ed. John Carey, Faber, 1987.
Firegrates and Kitchen Ranges, David J. Eveleigh, Shire Publications, 1983.

First Aid, The Authorised Manual of St John Ambulance Association and Brigade, 1975.

Food in History, Reay Tannahill.

Forensic Medicine, Professor Alan Watson, Gower, 1989.

Forgotten Household Crafts, National Trust.

Gray's Anatomy ed. P. L. Williams, Churchill Livingstone, 1989.

Have You Forgotten Yet?, Alan Delgado, David & Charles, 1973.

How They Lived, Vol. 3, 1700–1815, Asa Briggs, Blackwell, 1969.

Life of the Farm, The, Rintoul Booth, Peter Haddock Ltd, 1973.

New System of Domestic Cookery, A, 'A Lady' (Mrs M. Rundell), 1819.

Occupations, ed. Kathy Davis, HMSO, 1990.

Old Cooking Utensils, David J. Eveleigh, Shire Publications, 1985.

Penguin Dictionary of Historical Slang, Eric Partridge, 1980.

Pocket Dictionary of American Slang, The, Harold Wentworth & Stuart Berg Flexner, Pocket Books, USA, 1967.

Potholing and Caving, EP Publishing Limited.

Sainsbury's Book of Wine, Oz Clarke, Webster's Wine Guides, 1987.

Sea Slang of the 20th Century, W. Granville, Winchester Publications, 1949.

Sex in History, Reay Tannahill.

Weaker Vessel, The, Antonia Fraser, Methuen, 1984.

Places to visit

Brannan's Pottery, Barnstaple, N. Devon.
Castle Drogo, ten miles west of Exeter, Devon.
Dartington Crystal, Great Torrington, N. Devon.

Kedleston Hall, nr Derby, Derbyshire.
Lanhydrock House, nr Bodmin, Cornwall.
Poldark Mine and Heritage Centre, Wendron, nr Helston, Cornwall.
Uppark, SE of Petersfield, West Sussex.
Wellcome Historical Medical Museum, Euston Road, London.

Other

I'm All Right Jack, film.
The Lancet, medical journal.

A chain of shops called Past Times supplies many useful research items, for example a medieval cookbook with authentic recipes. There are cassettes of Middle Ages, Tudor and Anglo-Saxon music, eighteenth-century bawdy ballads, and music hall et cetera. There are Victorian parlour games, and a Victorian catalogue of household goods, and a host of other interesting items that would add credibility to a novel.

In the twentieth-century section, there are cassettes of Noël Coward songs and Winston Churchill's speeches, and a paperback called *Union Jack*, which is an anthology from the wartime troops' own daily newspapers 1939 to 1945.

Past Times supplies a postal catalogue and has a postal ordering service. Enquiries to Past Times, Witney, Oxfordshire, OX8 6BH, tel. 0993-779339. Some shop addresses are as follows: Brompton Road, Knightsbridge, London; Buchanan Street, Glasgow; Calverley Road, Tunbridge Wells; Castlegate, York; Frederick Street, Edinburgh; Princesshay, Exeter; South Street, Chichester; Westover Street, Bournemouth.

6

ACTIVITIES OF ORDINARY PEOPLE

It would be impossible to try to cover the enormous scope that this chapter title suggests. The activities of ordinary people are obviously diverse and sometimes extraordinary. From the fanatical collector of fine china to the petty crook, from the weekend caravanner to the armchair detective, hobbies and diversifications are part of the British way of life.

Information on such activities is readily available through specialist magazines, and a browse at any newsagents will provide you with enough copy to form a background for your novel. It would be more difficult to find a hobby that *doesn't* have a magazine devoted to it. If you need to find magazines that are available on, say, the teenage scene, a good source of reference is *The Writer's Handbook*. This lists the main teenage magazines which would contain all the relevant topics necessary to provide the background for a teenage novel, or any novel that included adolescents.

I want to reiterate here that my named sources in this chapter, as in all the others, comprise only a fraction of the thousands of books and outlets that can be used for research purposes for the novel. I stress again that this is necessarily an overview of all that is available, and that I have chosen what I consider to be some of the most useful sources, many of which I have used myself. Other authors will have very different lists but, hopefully, some of my choices can be added to them.

Many of the sections will overlap, and some may contain topics with which you may not agree. Do you consider witchcraft to be religion, for instance? It is reputedly the oldest religion in the world, and therefore some reference to it is included in this chapter. The activities of ordinary people cover such a wide range that only a selection of those that appear most frequently as the background or setting of novels can be included here.

Very often, nothing more than the mere flavour of an activity, to add to the personalities and lifestyles of the characters, is all that's required in a novel. In other cases, more detailed information to ensure the authenticity of the work will be essential. Much depends on the theme and scope of your novel, and on the kind of writer that you are.

I also suggest that you take note of the sources available, use them as starting points where applicable, and then expand on them. Most of the books mentioned will have bibliographies, in which a wealth of suggested further reading can be found. It's very short-sighted for a researcher to ignore this page. Very often, a book noted in the bibliography will yield as much, or more, valuable information than the original.

Fairs and rituals

Fairs and rituals have always been very much a part of British life, and many of them find their way into novels. Most visitor centres will have leaflets on any local fairs relevant to the area. Local and country fairs have traditionally celebrated anything and everything, from the ancient ritual of bringing in the harvest to the more contemporary annual Garden Festival of Wales, showing and preserving all that is special to the area.

The many steam fairs that are seen around the country in the summer months usually have a bonus section of old wagons, cars or motor cycles, and almost always there are displays of farming implements and machinery. And the most innocent of rural fairs with all its homely activities has been the background for many a fictional crime.

County fairs depicting the everyday activities of the people involved are one of the riches of the British way of life, and the researcher into country customs can do no better than to visit any one of them for the flavour and atmosphere of times past and present. It's not all jelly and jam-making, and an enjoyable day out is one of the perks of 'researching'.

Some quite common rituals that were practised by our ancestors have merged into the realm of superstition. The little locally published booklets on such themes that you see in holiday resorts and other places, can often provide enough detail to get the imagination going.

I have a collection of booklets from Cornwall, since much of my novel-writing has been set in that county. *Cornish Customs and Superstitions*, for instance, cost only twenty pence at the time of purchase, and gave me a wealth of information and anecdotes on the rituals of Christmas Eve, superstitious Midsummer customs and so on. *Cornish Folklore* continues on the same lines, and such booklets can be found in most of our towns and cities, and are within the range of every pocket.

Many country fairs have the useful sidelines of horse-trading and gypsy fortune-telling. If the ritual of a genuine gypsy life is what you're seeking for your novel, then *A Romany Life* by Gipsy Petulengro (my hardback copy, second-hand, cost me £3) is a fascinating autobiography on everyday bohemian life. It also contains many true Romany terms, rituals, anecdotes, and details of gypsy charms, for good or ill.

On a similar bohemian theme, a circus autobiography called

My Wild Life by Jimmy Chipperfield (hardback, second-hand £3) gives a marvellous insight into the world of the circus, both in the career of the circus performer, and the animal training that is so much a part of it. Born into a legendary circus family whose first recorded showman took a performing bear on to the frozen Thames in 1684, Jimmy Chipperfield takes you behind the scenes into a magical world that the average person never dreams about.

Another excellent autobiography, *Circus*, by Paul Eipper (hardback, second-hand £6), was published in 1931. This may account for the way the book is, rather oddly, written in the present tense, but the story is none the less vivid for all that. It too is not only very animal-orientated, but brings all the glitter and magic of the circus to life.

The above three books were found at Hay-on-Wye. For those who haven't yet visited the town, it's worth a mention that many of the second-hand bookshops have sections devoted to whatever topic you're looking for, which cuts down on the search time considerably. I have also found the assistants to be generally knowledgeable and helpful.

Courting, marriage customs, married life

Many historical novelists have added to the intrigue of their plots by the use of love potions and old legends and customs. In several of my early historical romances, I made up my own legends, based loosely on facts I discovered in old books on the ghosts and legends of certain areas.

A book that could easily be used to provide facts of this nature is *Love Potions* by Josephine Addison, subtitled *A Book of Charms and Omens*. From the amazing number of methods for one person to seduce another, whether or not you think they come into the realm of old wives' tales, there is ample scope for romantic novelists in search of such a theme. There are plenty of suggested aphrodisiacs, including the everyday lettuce on which Venus was said to have lain the body of her lover (one of the more peculiar snippets in the book . . .).

Superstitions in plenty can be found in this and similar books. Having a mole on your body is considered lucky. It is supposedly unlucky to pick a pansy sprinkled with dew, as it's meant to cause the death of a loved one. A useful tip for a wife wanting to be rid of her not-quite-so-loved husband, perhaps?

My favourite mini-book, bought for 50 pence, is called *The Folklore and Customs of Love and Marriage*, of which there were certainly plenty in days gone by. It covers courting rituals, the betrothal, variations on the wedding ceremony, bridal bouquets, the meanings of different-coloured wedding dresses, and much more. A mass of information to trigger the imagination of the most cynical romantic novelist (if there are any) can be found in this little book.

Another book covering topics of a wider nature is *A Collection of Old English Customs and Curious Bequests and Charities*. Phew. The wordy title alone might tell you this was written in 1842. It's unlikely to be found anywhere but second-hand bookshops, and may require quite a search. Having never found it yet, I'm not sure how much use it would be to a novelist.

Magazines dealing specifically with the contemporary marriage scene today, costs and so on, are *Brides and Setting up Home* and *Wedding and Home*. Most other women's magazines contain features of similar interest and information, and are cheap and easy research sources for background detail for contemporary novels.

Sports

It's hardly necessary to mention the masses of sporting magazines available, and books on every kind of sport imaginable can be easily found. A random sample includes *The Horse Rider's Handbook*, covering dressage, show jumping and cross-country riding. Or how about the *Hamlyn Encyclopedia of Boxing* if your book has a pugilistic background? This book includes biographies and statistics, as well as essential information on all kinds of boxing.

The children's library will contain simplified books on all kinds of sporting activities, or you may have already become an expert on the moves of snooker from your TV armchair. Television has brought every kind of sport right into our lives, and has probably provided authors with background ideas they would never have thought of before.

A cheap little paperback series such as the EP Sport Series will give you all you need to know about various sporting activities in a nutshell. These particular books may be out of print now, but similar ones will certainly have taken their place. I've had a book in this series for some years. It is called simply *Rock Climbing*, and from the information and advice in its pages I gave the characters in one of my books an authoritative rock-climbing adventure.

Among others in this particular series, under the general heading of KTG – Know the Game – were: *Track Athletics*, *Wildwater Canoeing*, *Golf*, *Start Motor Cruising*, *Conditioning for Sport* et cetera. It's always worth looking for these smaller and well-illustrated paperbacks, often found in sports shops as well as bookstores, since they give just as much information as a larger tome, and are usually written in a more reader-friendly way than some of the weightier volumes.

If hot-air ballooning takes your fictional fancy, then for atmosphere, statistics, and sheer adventure value I can thoroughly recommend a true account of the first balloon flight across the Atlantic. The book is called *Double Eagle*, and will make you think twice every time you see one of those pretty advertising balloons floating effortlessly in the sky.

I have never been up in a balloon, but while I was visiting Washington DC, I went to the Smithsonian Museum and saw a film called *To Fly*. So what? you may ask. Well, imagine sitting down to watch a film and the moderately sized screen in front of you suddenly expanding to virtually envelop the audience. Imagine the seats moving slightly in a way that makes you almost sea sick ... and imagine that through the magic of auto-suggestion and big-screen technology, you are suddenly, virtually 'in' the basket of a hot-air balloon and floating high in the sky.

Are you with me? I doubt it. You can't be, unless you've experienced it for yourself. Not until you have been in that extraordinary cinema and begun the most extraordinary simulated flight, and felt your stomach sink as you lurch over Niagara Falls in your balloon, or as you glide through the awesome magnificence of the Grand Canyon, soar over the skyscrapers of Manhattan, or the vast, sweltering wheat plains of middle America ...

If you get the chance to enjoy one of the many hands-on experiences which the Americans, in particular, do so well, don't miss it. Nearer to home, should tennis feature as the background of your novel, the Wimbledon Lawn Tennis Museum in London will provide you with the history of tennis, showing you some of the trophies, and including films of the most famous matches over the years. If you can't get to London, a stamped, addressed envelope with a query letter may provide you with pamphlets and details.

A hardback book I bought for 30 pence at a library sale is laboriously called *Canoeing Skills and Canoe Expedition Technique for Teachers and Leaders*. But that's where the heavy-handedness ends. Written in a crisp and informative way, it must contain virtually everything you could possibly need to know about the sport, and is lavishly illustrated. For the basics dos and don'ts of canoeing, I wouldn't need to look any further than this one book. There's just no point in spending so much time on the research that your book never gets written. Unless you enjoy the research more than the writing, of course . . .

Religion and politics

Whether or not you think that witchcraft as a religion comes into the scope of this chapter is up to you. As far as ritual goes, it certainly does. Our ancestors were pretty well governed by superstition, and the fascination of witchcraft lingers, whatever your feelings about the subject. I used it as a theme for one of my own novels, *Blackmaddie*, which I originally published as Rowena Summers in this country (Sphere and Severn House), and later as Jean Innes in the States (Zebra). There are many books available on witchcraft and the occult, and I was able to find an amazing number of such books in my comparatively small local library. They make such absorbing reading that you almost forget your intention is to research for your novel . . .

A lighthearted paperback to whet your appetite is *Witchcraft For All* by the supposedly Official Witch of Los Angeles, Louise Huebner. This is not in any way a heavy book, but can give an author endless ideas to use in novels ranging from romances to murder stories.

A far deeper and, in my opinion, creepier book is *Magic, Supernaturalism and Religion*, which gives a history of magical ideas and manifestations in the Western world. The author, Kurt Seligmann, the surrealist painter, examines the religio-magical beliefs of ancient and modern times. As a research tome, it is also well illustrated, but is not for the squeamish. Some of the subjects covered are Black Magic rites; astrology; vampires; secrets of the Bible; the principles of alchemy; omens and oracles; magic in Holy Writ; the Tarot; Masonic lodges; Christian Cabalists and the Jews; and the witch controversy in English literature. I've had the book on my shelf for several years, and have dipped into it occasionally, but I don't pretend to understand much of it. I merely list it as a research source if it would suit your kind of novel.

Specialist magazines for those interested in the occult and allied topics are *Prediction* and *Psychic News*, which is called 'the world's only spiritualist newspaper'. A subscription to this one would give you a good insight into psychic research, paranormal gifts, poltergeists, spiritual healing and so on. *Prediction* deals more with astrology as well as features with an occult slant.

A visit to the reference section of any library will show you the vast numbers of books on every kind of religion. Two of the more general ones are *Making Sense of Religion* by Donald Reeves, and *The World's Religions* by Ninian Smart. Cardinal Basil Hume's *Priesthood* tells of his own experience of priesthood.

Religious matters and background also feature in many specialist magazines, such as *Catholic Herald*, *Church of England Newspaper*, *The Tablet*, *Jewish Quarterly* and others. I suggest that if a specific religious background figures very highly in your novel, you talk to someone of that religion. I almost slipped up in one of my own books by quoting a phrase that a person of a particular faith wouldn't use, and was put right by checking with someone of that faith before I submitted the manuscript.

Religion and politics are not such strange bedfellows, when you consider how often the two have been involved over the centuries. A broad look at world politics since 1945 can be found in *The World Political Almanac* which is a source of factual information on the world's political events, organisations and personalities.

The House of Commons gives an illustrated introduction to the workings of the House, which is now also open to scrutiny on television. *British Political Facts 1900–1975* is a useful quick reference guide for further research into modern politics. *British National Archives* can be obtained free from HMSO. It is regularly revised and updated, and is a complete record of published official records.

Writing to your own or any other Member of Parliament or local government officer for specific information on a topic may yield pamphlets or a detailed letter, depending on the time available and the inclination of your correspondent. Sitting in on any local town hall debates or local council issues is a good way of absorbing the local political scene.

Becoming actively involved in any green belt, road-widening or housing issues, as I once did, will also give you an insight as to the lengthy proceedings and mass of paperwork to be waded through – and to the correctness of procedure and general wordiness of the QC appointed to your particular case. Access to such procedures is often right under our noses, and a look through any local newspaper will usually give you dates and times of such debates or public meetings. The general public is also often invited to attend local council proceedings.

It's possible for members of the public to sit in on many of the smaller court cases. This can be useful, not only to see what goes on in court, but also to define the pecking order of the officials. Such detail can be found readily enough in a reference book, and although I maintain that most research can be done quite successfully from an armchair, the unique atmosphere of a courtroom cannot easily be caught from a book. Much will depend on the case in question, and the temperament of the defendants and accusers. Being called to serve on a jury can be quite an eye-opener, and should not be overlooked as a source of research. You never know when you might need it for future reference.

Crime and punishment

Crime novelists obviously have a great responsibility to get things accurate. It's well worth searching through the second-hand bookshops for books on all grisly aspects of the subject of murder and mayhem. I am indebted to fellow writer, Stuart Drinkwater, for much of the information included here.

Recommended is the *Encyclopaedia of Murder* and the *Encyclopaedia of Modern Murder*. Both include excellent introductory essays on the subject of murder and motive. *Forensic Medicine* is for those with strong stomachs, as it is graphically illustrated. It is updated every five years, and generally regarded as a definitive teaching manual, and it is also used by eminent crime novelists for research. (Very expensive, Stuart Drinkwater's 1985 pb edition was £18).

Perhaps your novel is set in upmarket Hollywood, in which case a book called *Coroner to the Stars* might be useful, since it contains information on all kinds of glamour and gore in Tinseltown. *Forty Years of Murder* will give you an insight into the character and work of a then practising Home Office pathologist.

Drugs is a comprehensive volume covering the worries, threats and basic facts. It has many lists in easily recognisable chart form, covering identification and evidence of usage, and also lists the pop-scene names of drugs. *The Coward's Weapon* gives you the history of the many common and unsuspected poisons lurking in every garden and innocent hedgerow, with a good A-Z appendix listing them.

If you are looking for ideas from real-life crimes, then *Settings for Slaughter* covers thirteen macabre murders, and could be a real starting point for those suffering from murder-writer's block.

TV programmes such as *Lovejoy* and *Minder* take an almost benevolent view of rogues rather than criminals, but nevertheless give an insight into the workings of such a person's mind. Slightly more upmarket in the minor criminal league is *Perfect Scoundrels*, still grist to the mill for seeing how they get away with it. For fictional purposes, naturally . . .

Legal matters

Allied to the physical details of murder are legal matters and procedure. *The Crime Busters* covers the work of the FBI, Scotland Yard, Interpol and general criminal detection, and is a useful guide to historic background. *Police of the World* includes illustrations of uniforms. *Police* gives a good account of a police force at work, including details of Headquarters, the various uniforms, traffic, CID et cetera, and is very good for organisational requirements.

Or do as my friend in New York did, and go into any police station and ask questions, or ask to observe procedure. You may not be welcome on a busy day, but never forget the personal approach, and remember that most people are pleased to talk about their own work. And on a slack day, you may be very welcome indeed to break the monotony of a more general routine.

Information on police work and legal procedure is also available at the touch of a button on our TV screens. From *Kojak* and *The Bill* to *Heartbeat* and any programme covering court procedures, research is there for the taking. So are local and national newspapers, with their often gory detail of crimes and their follow-ups. In one report, I even read a detailed description of the last horrific moments of a condemned man in the electric chair. This was in an ordinary national newspaper, and is not the kind of information you come across every day. But if it interests you, your crime-cuttings file should certainly include that kind of reportage for future reference.

Relatively few of us, thank goodness, are familiar with the interior of a prison. It's simple enough to get the general idea of such interiors from any of the excellent documentaries that appear on our TV screens from time to time, or even from sitcoms such as *Porridge*. For more historical accuracy, various places are now open to the public, including Bodmin Jail. This is the former county prison of Cornwall, dating back to 1776, and you can visit the underground dungeons and also discover details of some of the crimes and punishments of our ancestors. Fascinating detail is provided for both the casual visitor and the researcher. It's probably not generally known that the Crown Jewels and the Domesday Book were stored here during the First World War. On view are the stocks and pillories, and the actual spot where the last public hanging in the country was performed in the early part of this century.

Specific book clubs such as the Crime Writers Club are an excellent way of building up your own research library. The many advertisements in Sunday newspaper supplements and the like will also give an illustrated spread of some of the books available. It's worth repeating that most book clubs make an initial offer of cheap books, but one of their conditions is that you then buy a certain number of books over a given period, usually a year. I never throw out mailshots without at least looking at them, because they may just contain something I want – and probably never knew I wanted . . . For instance, a book club with a wide range of titles is currently offering a useful reference book called *Guide to the Law*. Now that should be useful ... and yes, I've succumbed again.

But, as previously stated, book-club buying can ultimately work out very expensive, unless you intend writing a lot of books on a certain subject or period, and want to build up your own research library. If you don't want to splash out the money on buying the books that are advertised, you may find it useful to note the titles that are available, and then try your local library. If they don't have the book that you want in stock, they can usually order it for you.

Sources relevant to this chapter

Books (pub. date given where known)

A Collection of Old English Customs and Curious Bequests and Charities, H. A. Edwards, 1842.
A History of Everyday Things in England, Marjorie and C. H. B. Quennell, Batsford, 1984.
A Romany Life, Gipsy Petulengro, Devereux Books, 1935.
British National Archives, Government Publications Sectional List 24, HMSO, London.
British Political Facts 1900–1975, David Butler and Anne Sloman, Macmillan.
Canoeing Skills and Canoe Expedition Technique for Teachers and Leaders, Squadron Leader P. F. Williams RAF, Pelham Book, 1967.
Circus, Paul Eipper, Routledge, 1931.
Cornish Customs and Superstitions, Tor Mark Press, Truro.
Cornish Folklore, Tor Mark Press, Truro.
Coroner to the Stars, Thomas T. Noguchi, MD, Corgi, 1986.

Coward's Weapon, The, Terence McLaughlin, Robert Hale, 1980.

Crime Busters, The, edited by Angus Hall, Treasure Press, 1976.

Double Eagle, Charles McCarry, W. H. Allen, 1979.

Drugs, Dr Richard Barrymore, BCA, 1975.

Encyclopaedia of Modern Murder (1962–1982), Colin Wilson & Donald Seaman, BCA, 1984.

Encyclopaedia of Murder, Colin Wilson and Patricia Pitman, Pan, 1984.

Folklore and Customs of Love and Marriage, The, Margaret Baker, Shire Publications, 1974.

Forensic Medicine, Keith Simpson CBE and Bernard Knight, Edward Arnold, 1985.

Forty Years of Murder, Keith Simpson, Granada Publishing, 1978.

Hamlyn Encyclopedia of Boxing, Hamlyn, 1989.

Horse Rider's Handbook, The, Monty Mortimer, David & Charles, 1989.

House of Commons, The, John Biffen, Grafton, 1989.

Love Potions, Josephine Addison, Guild Publishing and BCA, 1987.

Magic, Supernaturalism and Religion, Kurt Seligmann, Allen Lane, 1971.

Making Sense of Religion, Donald Reeves, BBC Books, 1989.

My Wild Life, Jimmy Chipperfield, Macmillan, 1975.

Penguin Guide to the Law, The, John Pritchard, World Books, 1991.

Police, Clive Sturman, Purnell, 1981.

Police of the World, Roy D. Ingleton, Ian Allen Ltd, 1979.

Priesthood, Cardinal Basil Hume, Darton, Longman & Todd, 1989.

Rock Climbing, Dennis Kemp, EP Publishing, 1979.

Settings for Slaughter, Douglas Wynn, Futura, 1988.

Witchcraft For All, Louise Huebner, Tandem, 1971.

World Political Almanac, The, Chris Cook, Facts on File, 1989.
World's Religions, The, Ninian Smart, Cambridge, 1989.

Bookshop

Murder One, the Crime, Science Fiction and Romance
 Bookshop, 71-73 Charing Cross Road, London.

Magazines

Brides and Setting up Home
Prediction
Psychic News
Wedding and Home

Other

Bodmin Jail, Bodmin, Cornwall.
Garden Festival of Wales, annual, summer months.
London Dungeon, Tooley Street, London SE1.
Museum of Smuggling History, nr Ventnor, Isle of Wight.
To Fly, film, Smithsonian Museum, Washington DC, USA.
Wimbledon Lawn Tennis Museum, Church Street, London
 SW19.

7

THE PUBLIC LIVES OF IMPORTANT PEOPLE

It's an endless source of fascination to find out what makes other people 'tick', and to sneak a look into other people's lifestyles. One of the things that makes historical fiction so appealing is how the real historical figures successfully blend in with the characters the author creates. By bringing in these real people, the author immediately gains an extra dimension of reality. *Providing he gets it right.*

The important people in this world have very public images, and never more so than nowadays, when they can be brought right into our homes via the television screen, so it's essential that any mention of them should be correct. You can't afford to describe someone of stature as being small and puny when any library biography displays endless photographs of his girth and larger-than-life qualities. This may be taking things to extremes, and no author with any sense would be guilty of such a gaffe, but it's so easy to think we know something very well, then to describe it in a novel without checking, and get it totally wrong.

As a brief example, photographs of Prince Charles's sons are legion. But could you give a snap reply as to the colour of their eyes? Or say at once which of the current crop of top snooker players is left-handed? (This would be an easy one only for snooker followers.) You may never want to mention either of these things – but if you do, then you would need to check your royal sources, and make sure you don't let Jimmy White pot the black ball from his right-hand side.

Researching historical personalities

So much has been written about historical personalities that it's hard to avoid reading about the latest biography or autobiography. But making use of them for fictional purposes means being accurate to your sources, and being careful to avoid saying anything slanderous or detrimental about them.

When I wrote about Bonnie Prince Charlie, as I did in *Scarlet Rebel* (Jean Saunders, Severn House), it was necessary for the atmosphere of the scene to describe his appearance when he first appeared on Scottish soil. To depict him as anything other than the slight, fair-haired man that he was would have been false. In this case, it hardly mattered that his physical appearance wasn't that of a giant, since he was already a giant in spirit to those awaiting him. But I couldn't have made him physically so, just for the sake of the book. You can't bend history to suit your story. The following sections tell you some of the best ways of researching well-known people with as much accuracy as possible.

Biographies

Biographies are obviously helpful in describing appearances and personalities in detail, since the author will have an objective opinion of his subject. Apart from the inevitable photographs, *auto*biographies often avoid descriptions of physical appearance. After all, it's hard to relate in the first person that 'I am young, blonde and beautiful . . .' when a TV appearance may show only too obviously that the lady is well past her prime. The autobiographer will understandably have a biased view of his or her own personality, and any photographs chosen for the book will be of the most flattering. Not all autobiographers will be narcissistic, but you should be aware that they might be.

It's as well to consult several biographies if your subject is to appear in any detail in your novel. I have always found the most useful ones are those that are lavishly illustrated, so that you can fix in your mind a variety of pictures of your subject in different circumstances. Among the readily available biographies that I have used are those on Abraham Lincoln, Florence Nightingale, Queen Victoria and Isambard Kingdom Brunel. There is no shortage of such books in any library, and new ones about political leaders and pop stars, and, especially, royalty seem to appear almost daily.

These real people, and others that I have written about, have sometimes played no more than a peripheral part in my novels, but it was essential to get their descriptions and manners correct. I own reference books on most of my subjects, as they have tended to crop up more than once in my novels, and therefore I think the expense of buying them is worthwhile. But you may justifiably argue that if the real people are to play only a small part in your novel, there is no need to buy expensive books. In that case, a visit to any public library with a notebook can probably give you all the detail you need.

In one of my historical novels I wanted to describe my hero as being physically like Prince Albert. In fact, when the heroine first sees him, she thinks for a moment that he *is* the prince. By describing the handsome royal features in this instance, the reader got an indirect description of the hero at the same time. Several photographs of the well-known features of Prince Albert gave me all that I required.

But not all biographies concern royalty and historical figures.

Many have been written about show-business people and sportsmen, and can give a useful background to a novel featuring such fictional characters. As an example, a double biography depicting the rise of a famous musical duo is Frederick Nolan's *The Sound of Their Music*, detailing the show-business lives of Rodgers and Hammerstein.

Historical accuracy

One thing you should always ascertain is that your real person can be where you said he/she was at a given time. In one of my early books, *The Whispering Dark* (Jean Innes, Robert Hale), I wanted my hero to meet Isambard Kingdom Brunel, and from my research material I made sure that the great engineer would be in Bristol at that particular time. Further, I ensured that he often frequented the waterside inns, where my artist hero was also usually to be found, to sketch.

Nothing infuriates a reader more to discover that an author has got it wrong. Whether or not the average reader would even know, or suspect such a thing, seems to me to be irrelevant. For your own integrity and satisfaction, you should always aim to get it right. So it takes a little time. Or sometimes a great deal of time . . . But it will be worth it in the end when readers say how fascinated they were by all the little details in your book – and *you* know that those details were correct.

Letters and diaries

The situation is somewhat different if your novel revolves almost entirely around a noted historical personality. You may want to put actual words into his mouth, and to avoid the risk of living relatives descending on you for defamation of character. In this case, an autobiography will suit you admirably, particularly where it gives instances of letters and diary entries, such as my volume of *Queen Victoria, Her Life and Times*, vol. 1, which covers the period from 1819 to 1861.

Who can dispute the recorded diary entries included here? And Queen Victoria, like many of her subjects, was an avid diary and letter writer. It's not difficult to track down such sources, and by doing so, you will certainly get beneath the skin of the historical character you're writing about through her own words and feelings.

It was from this book (and one or two others) that I picked up a gem of a passage about the ghastly mishaps at Queen Victoria's coronation. I already knew of one or two, but in reading her own comments and those of the narrative, I got some further ideas for scenes in my novel *A Royal Summer* (Sally Blake, Mills & Boon Masquerade). This is one of the bonuses of research. You look up one thing, and you find many more that you can use.

Some books of a similar nature to the Queen Victoria volume are listed below, but there are vast numbers of others readily available, and a query at your library will produce the information you require. The literary works of a dual-role personality, such as Sir Winston Churchill, can also give an insight into his or her character that you may wish to use.

Sometimes an author will create a novel based on the life of an historical figure. The lifestyle of someone like Elizabeth Barrett Browning, for instance, or the more contemporary Amy Johnson, would provide enough drama and emotional content to satisfy any reader. But how true to the original you could go is debatable. Do you acknowledge that this is based *On The Life Of* . . .? This is up to the individual to decide. It may be enough simply to utilise and adapt their experiences for a novel.

However, if you copy and/or fictionalise real lives too closely, despite using different names, you should state quite frankly in the frontispiece that this was your intention. Successful novels have been based on the lives of historical people, true crimes or supernatural occurrences.

My own gut reaction to all this is that historical data is best used as a background basis, and that a novelist should then use the imagination to elaborate and embellish the ideas gained from such research. For a straight historical novel, if you follow the recorded facts about a well-known figure too faithfully, 'where only the names have been changed', the danger is that you may just end up writing another thinly disguised biography.

Allowing your fictional characters to meet and talk with real people is certainly one of the ways of giving your novel more authority, and also gives added interest to the story. Shortly after the death of the Duchess of Windsor, there was a great explosion of information about the Duke and Duchess and many letters to and from the couple were published. Since these were then put into the public domain, it follows that a novel in which the characters were confidantes of the royal couple could presumably be familiar with such intimate details about their life.

Political events, whether or not they involve royal figures, have always provided a rich source of background around which to weave fiction. The abdication of Edward VIII changed the course of British history, and this fact in itself has been enough to intrigue more than one fiction author.

It's always worth saving any nuggets of information about such events and putting them into a special file. In a future novel, for instance, you may want to feature very close fictional friends of the royal couple who might know the terms with which they addressed one another. Your characters may be invited to a country-house weekend at which the royal couple are present. Or they may have once met the Duke, and feel mortified at his eventual situation, feeling that they 'knew' him from that one chance meeting.

It's not my intention to supply plot ideas, merely to show how the very fact of 'doing the research' can trigger the imagination. But in any of the above situations, your writing would have a far greater feeling of authenticity if you could incorporate some little anecdote that had been reported in a published memoir.

Family assistance

If the subject you are including in your novel is of a more contemporary vintage, letters, diaries and memoirs may be available from the family. But this can be a tricky case, and you may come up against strong family opposition. Is a novel *per se* worthy of a family exposing a loved one's innermost thoughts? It probably all depends on the novel, the author, and the integrity with which you wished to use the information.

At the very least, I suspect you would be asked to describe the theme of the novel thoroughly, and you may be requested to present for the family's approval those passages of your novel that include the personal detail.

Detailed information of this kind is more normally confined to non-fiction and further biographies. I would only say that if you go to the considerable trouble of this kind of research, approach the family tactfully, and don't make mistakes in your interpretation of the facts. But wherever and however you bring a real person into your novel, there are a few basic rules to remember:

- Don't put words and opinions into your real people's mouths that they would never dream of saying.

- Don't dress them in styles that would offend them, or are wrong for their period.
- Don't put them in places they couldn't possibly be at any given time, when history records them as being elsewhere.
- Don't dramatise any of their life-or-death scenes to suit your novel.
- Don't elaborate on any scandal that can't be readily confirmed by recorded history.

Visual aids

Into this category come the many exhibitions around the country depicting the lives of important people. Since the long reign of Queen Victoria is probably one of the most used periods for the historical novelist, I make no apology for again referring to the lady in this context. One of the most successful and interesting exhibitions to get an instant picture of pomp and ceremony is the Royalty and Empire Exhibition at Windsor Central Station.

Such a visit can also be combined with one to Windsor Castle, which is an easy stroll away. Parts of the castle are open to visitors, including the State Apartments, and also St George's Chapel, unless you're unlucky enough to go there on a day when it's closed for private purposes, as I did ... A phone call should establish this for you. Nearby is also The Royal Mews, where many of the state carriages are housed. However, since the fire that ravaged the castle in 1992, it will be some time before Windsor can be seen in its full glory again.

But would such detailed description of any of these things surrounding your royal figures be vital to your novel? These are the things you should weigh up before you go to the trouble of a day out to take you away from your writing.

Perhaps if you wanted to invent an aristocratic family using pseudo-royal carriages, and you wanted to know how to arrange it so that one of the wheels buckled and killed or maimed several of the occupants, or passers-by, it would be useful . . . Or if you are the kind of aesthetic writer who really needs to touch the upholstery or the gilt, or to smell the leather . . .

But if I only needed to 'see' the carriage to describe it for the purposes of including such a vehicle in your novel, then, quite frankly, I would go to the library and take out a book on the subject. In *A Royal Summer* I was able to describe Queen Victoria's coronation carriage perfectly adequately in this way.

Visual aids include films and TV documentaries. Many old films crop up regularly on TV, and many more are available on video, and can be hired cheaply. Some of the old films have certainly been accurate enough to use as a research source, since they obviously had researchers working for them in the first place. A small selection includes *Lady Hamilton*, *Lawrence of Arabia*, *Gandhi*, *Mary Queen of Scots*, *Scott of the Antarctic*, *Henry V* and *The Lady with the Lamp*.

While some of the older films may have taken certain liberties in their presentations, TV documentaries hopefully present a truthful picture. The frequency with which they occur on notable people is proof of the fascination of the wealthy and famous to the rest of us. Royalty, in particular, are always under the TV and media microscope, and never have we been given more of an insight into how such people live, their pastimes and even their incomes.

The history programmes of the Open University TV courses can be useful. So can the morning schools programmes, and the nostalgia programmes that deal with important personages. Also, whenever a 'personality' dies, a documentary of their life is shown with seemingly miraculous speed. This not only applies to royalty, but people in other walks of life, especially the entertainment field. Such personalities include the much-missed Frankie Howerd and Benny Hill, who died within a very short space of one another, and who both featured as documentary worthies.

Another kind of visual aid to research is Madame Tussaud's Waxwork Museum in London, and similar museums in other parts of the country. Here you will find lifelike models of murderers and sports stars, royalty and film stars, all rubbing shoulders with one another in all their pomp or gory detail. Weight, height, stature, physical peculiarities, facial characteristics, beauty or otherwise, are all there for the viewing.

Most of the stately homes around the country have booklets or biographies devoted to their owners, which are always worth buying and filing. You may not want to write specifically about Lord and Lady whoever, but you may want to invent fictional characters loosely based on that kind of lifestyle and background.

When any personality in the public eye marries, or dies, or is involved in any kind of scandal, you can be sure that the newspapers will have a field day. If one of these personalities – the late Robert Maxwell, or Marlene Dietrich, for example – interests you as a role model for a fictional character, it's a good idea to collect as many newspapers as possible at the time, and file all the relevant articles. This way you will get a comprehensive picture of the person, from the many different perspectives of reporters, family members, acquaintances and hangers-on.

You can be sure that people will metaphorically be coming out of the woodwork to give their particular opinion on the person, and there will never be a better time to collect a fully rounded picture of his/her vices and virtues than when the story is white hot. Every newspaper and magazine will want to be the first to present some new and hitherto 'unknown' facts or give some dastardly secrets away.

This is the ideal time for the researcher to cash in on those free insights into the lives of the rich, the famous and the infamous, and to file them away for future use. Later on - and quite often remarkably soon after the event - an informed biography will undoubtedly appear. But however good it may be, those on-the-spot and at-the-time articles will give you a greater variety of personal views on your subject than a single official biographer ever could.

Interviewing

When you want to include some famous person who is still alive in your novel, you are perfectly at liberty to mention them by name, or to comment on their appearance, or to suggest that your characters attended the same event, such as Badminton, when Princess Anne might be competing.

If the person's appearance in the plot is slight and would cause no detriment or embarrassment, then there's no need to acquaint him with your intention. But you may want to bring him into your novel in an important capacity, by putting him into some controversial discussion, for instance. In this case, you should be very sure of his views, or you could find yourself involved in a libel case. The easiest way out of this is to ask your subject's permission to include him in your novel, and this you should do in writing.

A letter is not so much an intrusion into a busy person's day as a telephone call, and doesn't put him or her on the spot. If he has to give you an instant answer on the telephone, it is more likely than not to be a refusal - better to give him time to peruse your request in a letter. Would your minor nobility want to be included in a romantic novel, for instance? Would your TV celebrity want to be associated with your fictional crook who inveigles himself into the celebrity's game show in order to gain access to whatever? I'm merely suggesting here all the pros and cons that your celebrity might consider.

It's obvious from this that you should give him/her some idea of what your novel is about, and how s/he is going to figure in it. It's highly unlikely that any celebrity is going to relish being shown up in a bad light, or in being conned, and if this is your intention, it's far better to keep all the characters fictional in the first place.

And if you get written permission from your celebrity to use his name in a scene in your novel, keep his reply in a safe place, just for insurance. You never know when you might need it.

Face-to-face technique

A request for a personal interview with an important person to get some background into their family history for your novel's sake should also be in writing in the first instance. You should state all the reasons given above, briefly listing any credentials such as your own writing CV, and your interest in this particular subject. Be polite and tactful, and include a SAE for a reply.

When it comes, and you get the coveted interview, arrive on time, and don't go in armed with a camera and tape-recorder at the ready. By all means, have these things discreetly available, but ask if you may use them, and be ready to have permission refused, especially about the tape-recorder. Many people hate the things, in which case you will have to rely solely on your own written notes. But if someone has agreed to be interviewed, it's hardly likely that they'll object to your taking notes. Offer to have your source acknowledged in your novel when it's published, and if this is accepted, don't forget it.

It's worth mentioning a few points about the actual face-to-face interviewing technique, especially if your interviewee is an older person, such as an elderly domestic employee or retired children's nanny, or gardener. However nervous you are, it's possible he may be even more nervous, especially if the appointment has been arranged for some time. You at least have the background of your novel in your mind, while he may well be more than a mite suspicious of your motives in questioning him. Those miserable kiss-and-tell 'novels' are all too prominent nowadays.

Aim to reassure him as quickly as possible as to why you're there, otherwise you're unlikely to get much out of him. Explain a little about your work, though not too much. An interview should not be an exercise in displaying all your working methods, nor giving away your plot. You should especially explain that your purpose is not to expose family secrets, but to get to know the background of your subject a little better so that you can portray him in as sympathetic a light as possible.

In other words, get your interviewee on your side. Don't be aggressive or persistent, especially, if there are obvious areas he doesn't care to answer. An uncomfortable interviewee will dry up faster than blinking. Save those thorny questions for the next person you talk to, if any.

The person you want to interview may live too far away for reasonable access. In which case, you will need to request your information in writing, again always enclosing a SAE. Ask first if your interviewee would mind answering certain questions, and list them properly on a separate sheet of paper, rather than including them in your letter in a random way. Be professional, but be tactful.

You should always aim to be seen as a responsible interviewer, even if this is not your real forte. And, let's face it, it's more often journalists rather than novelists who go out and interview people. But there's nothing like a snippet of real information for creating an authentic atmosphere in a work of fiction, from someone 'who was there', or who actually worked in any given occupation of which you have no knowledge.

Supposing you intend to interview, say, ten people about your subject. Then you should be ready, either verbally or in writing, with the same list of questions. That way, you will again get a fully rounded piece of information to each question.

If ten answers agree, you can be pretty sure it's accurate. If they don't, you will have to choose what seems to be the most likely character assessment or factual point. Or you can decide to leave the detail out altogether. As a novelist, don't forget you always have that option.

Sources relevant to this chapter

Books (pub. dates given where known)

Abraham Lincoln, Lord Longford, BCA, 1974.
Florence Nightingale, Elspeth Huxley, Chancellor Press, 1975.
Florence Nightingale, Norman Wymer, OUP.
Isambard Kingdom Brunel, L. T. C. Rolt, BCA, 1972.
Letters and Documents of Napoleon, John Eldred Howard, OUP.
Life and Times of Elizabeth I, The, Neville Williams, BCA, 1972.
Life and Times of George V, The, Denis Judd, BCA, 1972.
Life and Times of Victoria, The, Dorothy Marshall, BCA, 1972.
Lives of the Indian Princes, Charles Allen, Century Publishing, 1984.
Men Who Ruled India, The, Philip Woodruff.
Queen Victoria and the Bonapartes, Theo Arunson, Cassell, 1972.

Queen Victoria, Her Life and Times, Vol. I 1819–1861, Cecil Woodham-Smith, BCA, 1973.
Richard Burton, My Brother, Graham Jenkins, Sphere, 1988.
The Sound of Their Music, The Story of Rodgers & Hammerstein, Frederick Nolan, Unwin, 1978.

Films

Gandhi
Henry V
Lady Hamilton
Lawrence of Arabia
Mary Queen of Scots
Scott of the Antarctic
The Lady with the Lamp

Exhibitions

Beatle City, Albert Dock, Liverpool.
Madame Tussaud's Waxwork Museum, Marylebone Road, London.
Royalty and Empire Exhibition, Central Station, Windsor.

Other

Open University TV programmes.
Schools TV programmes.
TV 'personality' documentaries.

8

INFLUENCE OF HISTORICAL EVENTS

World and national events

Using world or national events as a background is one of the most useful ways of creating parameters for your book. I have used the period of the First World War, the Indian Mutiny, the Crimean War and the Jacobite Rebellion, among many other large-scale backgrounds, and in each case those world events gave me a useful time-guide against which to plot my story.

The influence of world events in all our lives is such that they create a sense of drama in themselves, and therefore are tailor-made to provide authentic background detail for the historical novelist. More recently, the Falklands War and the Gulf War have all created their own lure for the author who wants to blend dramatic fact and fiction.

Many political, social and royal events too have provided scope for books and films. The abdication of Edward VIII changed the course of royal history for Britain, and was always destined to be a fascination for writers of fact and fiction. I've previously mentioned the emotional newspaper articles containing the letters between him and the Duchess, which showed the human side of the turmoil. But you also need to have an objective view if you're to write about such an event in any detail.

A useful little book that I found, which was far less emotional than many others on this subject, was *The Abdication of King Edward VIII* by Lord Beaverbrook. This book provides a day-by-day record of the crisis as Lord Beaverbrook saw it, and makes choice reading about 'informed sources'. The book includes the way the Press handled the affair, including the various reports, denials, and arguments, from intimates of the King – and much more besides.

Historical tragedies and scandals have always produced larger-than-life figures. Our own national history is a hot-bed of intrigue and poignancy and is, dare one say it, rich fodder for the novelist. You shouldn't twist history to suit your novel, and you'd be very foolish to risk writing up a recorded historical drama exactly as it happened, but you can certainly invent characters and situations to mirror them.

Seeking out intriguing little details can be both interesting and productive, since you will inevitably find out far more than you realised. The mere fact of researching into such world and national events can provide you with more than a solid background to your novel. It can also influence and aid the path of your plot and the development of your characters, and is one of my own favourite ways of constructing my novels.

But obviously not all world events were disasters. During the nineteenth century, in particular, there was much emigration to America and Australia, particularly in search of a new life and in expectation of gold-rush riches. A useful series under the umbrella title of Great Emigrations includes: *The Irish to North America*, *The Scots to Canada*, *The British to the Antipodes*. I bought my own copy of *The English to New England* in a WH Smith sale for 95 pence, and I suspect that most of the books are to be found second-hand or in libraries.

A book I haven't yet tracked down, but have had recommended to me, is *Keesing's Archives, a Weekly Diary of World Events*. It's in several volumes, beginning in 1931 and going up to the present day. That's all I know about it. If anyone can tell me any more details, I'd be obliged!

The Second World War

There's no doubt that battles and wars provide a very useful background in which to set a novel. What more convenient way can there be for an author to be rid of all the undesirables in his book, and to show the strengths and weaknesses of his characters, whether they are those at the front, or those left at home to work and pray?

History books are an obvious source of information for chronological detail about any war or individual battle. I have bought many second-hand books on this subject, as well as newer ones, and many reprinted old newspapers, mainly bought from the appropriate theme centres.

A reprinted old newspaper giving first-hand reactions to the Blitz, or photographs of end-of-the-war street parties, or the appearance of King George VI and Queen Elizabeth (now the Queen Mother) on the balcony of Buckingham Palace before a multitude of deliriously happy and cheering people, is worth far more to the novelist, in my opinion, than a dry old tome of a book giving no more than statistics. But unfortunately, you need those statistics in order to date and locate your novel correctly. The one source gives you the human aspect, but the other gives you the locations and parameters you need.

A useful book to be found in the children's library covering many battles is *Great Moments in Battle* by Ronald W. Clark, which covers all the great battles from Custer's Last Stand of 1876 to the Korean War of 1951.

My best 50-pence second-hand find at a library sale was a book on the American Civil War called *Civil War in Pictures*, again one of my favourite illustrated books. This one consists mainly of text and pictures from the drawing boards of the newspaper artists who recorded the conflict, and was hopefully as accurate as possible in an age before photography. A useful little children's book is called *American Civil War Wargaming*, and shows all the battles and uniforms of the protagonists in great pictorial detail.

But since the Second World War is the most recent world war in our history, it probably figures most often in novels, which is why I've singled it out in this section. The war is still within living memory, and many older people will remember those days, and almost everyone will have family members who were involved in some way, and can give you personal experiences. Family attics can be great sources of forgotten memorabilia, and a rummage through one of those old boxes can often produce treasures.

Without even going outside my own family circle, I could get first-hand information, or handed-down records and notes, on a variety of activities and experiences. They include the Home Guard and Civil Defence; the Navy; a tank regiment; the Royal Air Force; the London Blitz and the Bristol Blitz; doodlebugs; children's evacuation; the effects of deaths of friends and neighbours; near-misses in air raids; sleeping in cupboards under the stairs; or in shelters; or in the London Underground; the treatment and trauma of unexploded bombs, including one on my grandmother's London doorstep; and the exciting arrival of the Yanks in our quiet Somerset town.

All this, and I haven't even thought farther afield than within my own and my family's experiences. It makes sense to make use of what is readily available. You have to start somewhere, so don't always think you must spend days and weeks in libraries when the trigger to what you need for your novel may be much closer at hand than you think.

Television programmes frequently show documentaries and

old news programmes on the Second World War, especially as the various anniversaries come around. The Pathe News Video series includes a video for every year from 1930 to 1969, and the ones covering the years of 1939 to 1945 show all the major events of each year of the war in detail.

On video, you can obviously see the events in action, but far cheaper, and more readily to hand for reference than the videos, is a set of six hardback books which I bought for the amazingly low price of £3 in a small second-hand bookshop. The set is called *The War in Pictures*, and each volume gives comprehensive detail of daily or monthly activity in all aspects of the war, with detailed accompanying text.

A query among family and friends for 'research books' that may be mouldering in cupboards or in those attics has often produced surprises. Knowing I was interested in researching this particular war, a family member happily handed over to me three huge volumes from a set of books called *The War Illustrated*. Each volume consists of sequential editions of a weekly wartime magazine of the same name, and therefore goes into intense textual detail, as well as giving many illustrations, maps and plans, relevant drawings and diagrams. It proved to be of immense value to me.

One section of each magazine issue was an item called 'Our Diary of the War', giving a weekly rundown of the main areas of conflict et cetera. Another was a vastly useful and important feature called 'I Was There', subtitled 'Eye Witness Stories of the War'. It was from this source that I got a comprehensive list of food ration quantities and clothing coupon values, as well as reports of personal traumas and experiences.

The volumes were real treasures to find within my own family circle. If you want information about the Second World War and can track down any of them in second-hand bookstores, I thoroughly recommend them.

For sheer nostalgic reminiscences and more domestic personal experiences of the Second World War, I have two other books that have proved especially useful. One is *The Home Front*, whose contents reflect the title of the book, since it deals with civilian life in wartime. It includes economy tips from women's magazines, government handouts, details about air raids, Morrison shelters, munitions factories and so on. Much of it is written in personal anecdotal or diary form.

The other book is *No Time to Wave Good-Bye*, and contains the remembered reminiscences of Britain's wartime evacuee children. It makes poignant and revealing reading to learn how those children were bundled off to foster homes 'for the duration', each tagged with a luggage-label, and carrying a gas-mask in a brown cardboard box, and is a researcher's gem of a book. And, I warn you, it can make you weep.

Among useful books that may be found in children's libraries are *Catapulting from Colditz and Other Incredible Escapes*, which is as its title implies. And *This is Your War* gives a brief chronology of the main events, and consists mainly of Home Front propaganda. Included is a good bibliography for further reading on the subject.

One further book recommendation is *Invasion!*, a good value and highly illustrated paperback of the D-Day story, priced at £1.95.

During the Second World War, groups of people were asked to keep records of their own observations and comments for future use as research data. These observations are largely unpublished memoirs, and are now held in the Mass-Observation Archive at Sussex University. A letter or telephone call will provide details of their current accessibility.

If you have the time and opportunity, a visit to the Cabinet War Rooms in London will amaze you. Constructed and master-minded just prior to the war, it's a maze of underground, bomb-proof rooms where the Cabinet and Chiefs of Staff conducted 'their' war on our behalf. It is now virtually a time capsule of that organisation, and many of its 70 rooms are open to the public.

Uniforms, weaponry

You will obviously need to clothe all the military people in your novel, whether real or fictional, in the appropriate uniforms of their regiments and times. Many of the stately homes that have the clothes collections previously mentioned, also display coronation robes and the military attire of their owners and predecessors. The booklets describing the interiors and collections in such places can provide useful quick reminders of the uniforms on display.

It's just as important to give your characters the correct guns and weapons to take into battle with them. Again, a visit to a stately home, or a castle with a long historical background such as Warwick Castle, is probably the easiest way of seeing these things at a glance. Many of these places have gun-rooms and armouries and booklets that further describe their use.

But not everyone can afford the time, or is able, to make such visits. It's always worth writing to the publicity department of a house or castle that you think can help, and requesting any free pamphlets or information they can supply. Always enclose SAEs. And since you're more likely to get the freebies if they think you're going to spend money as well (which you probably are), ask the price of their current booklet or guide book and the postage required for them to send it to you by mail. It's tactful to say that you're writing a novel, and this is why you think the information they can supply would be immensely useful. A little honest flattery never hurt anyone.

* * *

One of the Time Life series of books called *The Gunfighters* gives plenty of detail about the guns of the old West, including when they were manufactured and used. If the Western is your theme, then you might seek out *Uniforms and Equipment of the Apache Wars*.

For a complete history of weaponry, from primitive bows and arrows to the sophistication of neutron bombs and laser-controlled missiles, *Firepower* by Philip Warner should give you all you need to know. The huge number of books available on war and all its aspects couldn't possibly be listed here, and I have only been able to select a very few, but I hope they will give you some idea of what to look for.

Local history and riots

It's often very tempting to new writers to tackle a novel on the huge scale, encompassing events in countries they know little about, and becoming totally bogged down in so much research that the novel never even gets off the ground. I hope that in the information on sources I've provided so far, it's realised that the most obscure facts can eventually be discovered and utilised. But these grand-scale scenarios don't necessarily make better books. Nor is it always necessary to spend time on researching fascinating detail on the Tuereg tribe of the Tunisian desert, for instance, which I hunted down for one of my own books (*Moonlight Mirage*, Sally Blake, Futura).

Your own home-grown local history can provide you with enough drama and detail to bring all the colour and richness of your characters to life – which is, after all, the main object of providing a strong and authentic background to any novel. Catherine Cookson proved this with her regional novels of the north-east. Other regional novelists have found the same thing. Many of my Rowena Summers novels were set in Cornwall or the West of England, which I know very well. Iris Gower sets hers in Wales, Margaret Thompson Davies in Glasgow, Marie Joseph in Lancashire, Susan Sallis in Gloucestershire, Elizabeth Daish on the Isle of Wight. And there are many more successful novelists who have looked inwards for research, rather than outwards.

None of the regional novels written by such authors takes its characters far beyond the boundaries of their home locations, unless the plot twists dictate it, but they all provide the reader with rich detail into the lives of the characters who lived there.

If you decide to do the same, then take note of the fact that it's not enough to chronicle trivial events, or your novel will be home-spun in the worst sense of the word. Base it on some local industry that you can research well. Or your characters could be involved in local riots or disturbances that will have a profound effect on them, and on your storyline. Wars will inevitably touch your community, with all the ensuing problems and poignancy.

Your local newspaper archives will probably have all the information you need on relevant events over past decades. Books on your own home town will tell you of the local characters who have made names for themselves in the past. Town and County museums will provide you with further information. Involve your museum curator in your project. They are usually very knowledgeable and happy to talk.

Books on local folklore, myths and legends can provide many ideas for novels, and can often point your plot in a solid direction. Rhona Martin's award-winning *Gallow's Wedding* was built around the ancient folklore than you could buy a man from the gallows, providing you agreed to take responsibility for him.

Natural and other disasters

The most absorbing kind of fictional reading is always larger than life, while reflecting all that is best and worst in it, so using natural and other disasters as a backdrop is a marvellous device to use, whether it is the pivot of a novel, the finale, or the point at which the novel begins.

I used a natural disaster at the start of *All in the April Morning* (Jean Saunders, W. H. Allen/Zebra USA). The book began with the San Francisco earthquake of 1906, and the traumatic experience affected the whole life of the main character who was involved in it.

My initial source of information on the earthquake was a book I bought on Paddington Station for £1.99, simply called *The World's Worst Disasters of the Twentieth Century*. Seven pages of this book were devoted to that earthquake, including illustrations, and provided almost all I needed to know. It helped that I had been to San Francisco, and knew the great undulations of the city hills, but even that wouldn't have been necessary. If you've ever seen a film about San Francisco, you would know it. If you've ever watched the TV series *The Streets of San Francisco* you would know it. If you remember it quite well just through my mentioning such visual sources, then you will realise how good a trigger your own memory is. And failing all that, any travel brochure in any travel agent's would give you pictures of the city's geography. But this comes into another chapter . . .

An earthquake is a natural disaster, along with volcanic eruptions, typhoons, floods, hurricanes and so on. Human-induced disasters, whether intentional or not, include oil-rig disasters, plane crashes and hi-jacks, bush fires, stock-exchange crashes, chemical leaks, government crashes, depressions, and business failures. And the list goes on.

Museums

There are vast numbers of museums around the country that are excellent sources of research. Among these are the many military museums, often with hands-on experiences for the benefit of the regular visitor, but which are of even more use to the researcher.

Eden Camp, in North Yorkshire, was once a prisoner-of-war camp, and now contains much Second World War memorabilia, and has various exhibitions. As I have already mentioned, these include the 'experience' of apparently entering a submarine, with all its accompanying noises, atmosphere and visual effects.

Such museums are numerous up and down the country. The Fleet Air Arm museum at Yeovilton houses aircraft past and present, with exhibits ranging from the First World War, the twenties and thirties, simulator experiences in a helicopter, naval jet, and another underwater 'experience' with sight and sound effects from a 1940 aircraft crash-landing on a Norwegian fiord.

This is only a small part of what this museum holds, and is typical of the sort of useful research information that is repeated in many others, a selection of which is listed below. As in the cases of the stately homes, if you are unable to visit, it's always worth sending a letter with SAE to the museum that may be of use to you, requesting information, or the prices of any booklets available by post. At the very least, you'll probably receive the museum's advertising leaflet, which will probably be enough to tell you whether you want to pursue it further.

Making the most of your research

The very availability of so many sources of research for what may be only a small proportion of your novel can be overwhelming. For the benefit of those who are new to novel-writing, I want to add a word of caution.

Make full use of any interesting information you find, but relate it in your own words in your novel – or in the words of your characters. This especially applies to historical speeches and even to informal dialogue. Don't copy your historical person's speech verbatim – *unless* this is part of your plot, and the person is actually saying the words in a particular scene in your novel.

If you were relating Lord Chamberlain's message on the advent of the Second World War, you would obviously want to detail it word for word if your characters were listening to it on the wireless. In such circumstances, it would be vital to include the speech verbatim for authenticity.

And if, for instance, your characters were present at Queen Victoria's coronation, and close enough to hear her responses, you would let your characters 'hear' her actual words. But if you simply wanted to use the information for your characters to discuss later, you would make the dialogue their own. They could refer to whatever your historical person said or did, and comment on it. But by then it would have become hearsay, and could be legitimately distorted in your characters' dialogue.

Your research doesn't have to be all used up in one novel, and this is why I never think it's a waste of money to collect as many books as you can afford on a subject that interests you. The Great Exhibition of 1851 has already figured to a greater or lesser degree in three of my novels. Much of the information, ascribed to Queen Victoria's recorded dialogue and diaries, was found in the aforementioned *Queen Victoria*, by Cecil Woodham-Smith.

In my novels involving the Great Exhibition, the background and description of the site, including the building of the Crystal Palace, the enormous interior, and the opening ceremony in the presence of Queen Victoria and Prince Albert, occurred most visually in *Willow Harvest* (Rowena Summers, Sphere/Severn House), when my rural characters took their basketware to exhibit. The experiences of my characters in London, where they were initially so clumsy and ill at ease, became one of the pivotal scenes in the book.

I used the exhibition more briefly as a time and location reference in *Lady of Spain* (Sally Blake, Mills & Boon Masquerade), when my Spanish wine-makers delivered their produce to London for the exhibition. In this case, I didn't take my characters inside the place, but it pin-pointed the hero's reason for being in London at all at that time.

Thirdly, the wonderful, shimmering interior of the Crystal Palace provided a sensual background description of richly hued embroidered Indian silks for my heroine to see and touch in *Golden Destiny* (Jean Saunders, Pocket Books, USA/Severn House).

These novels were all very different in plot and treatment, but they all made use of the same basic research source, whether it was just a starting point or a major turning point in the fortunes of the characters. There was far more research to do, since the other locations in the novels were also very different, ranging from the Somerset Levels to southern Spain to India and the Mutiny. But the Great Exhibition was an integral part of each book and three novels for the price of one lot of research is something I consider good value.

Sources relevant to this chapter

Books (pub. dates given where known)

Abdication of King Edward VIII, The, Lord Beaverbrook, 1966.

A Dictionary of World War II, James Taylor and Anne Wheal, Grafton.

American Civil War Wargaming, Terence Wise, Airfix Products Ltd, 1977.

British to the Antipodes, The, Jill Kitson, Gentry Books, 1976.

Catapulting from Colditz and Other Incredible Escapes, John L. Foster, Ward Lock Educational.

Civil War in Pictures, Fletcher Pratt, Garden City, NY, 1955.

English to New England, The, Douglas Hill, Gentry Books, 1975.

Firepower, Philip Warner, Grafton Paperbacks, 1989.

Great Moments in Battle, Ronald W. Clark, Phoenix House Ltd.

Home Front, An Anthology 1938–1945, The, edited by Norman Longmate, Chatto & Windus, 1981.

How We Lived Then: A History of Everyday Life during the Second World War, Norman Longmate, Hutchinson, 1971.

Invasion!, edited by Sir Larry Lamb, Express Newspapers, 1984.

Irish to North America, The, Frank Delaney, Gentry Books, 1976.

Keesing's Archives, a Weekly Diary of World Events.

Language of World War II, The, H. W. Wilson Co., New York, 1948.

Living Through the Blitz, Tom Harrison.

No Time to Wave Good-bye, Ben Wicks, Bloomsbury, 1988.

People's War, The, Angus Calder.

Reaching for the Skies, Ivan Rendell, BBC Publications, 1988.

Scots to Canada, The, Douglas Hill, Gentry Books, 1976.

This Is Your War, Marion Yass, HMSO, 1983.

Uniforms and Equipment of the Apache Wars, E. Lisle Reed-stom, Blandford, 1989.

War Illustrated, The, edited by Sir John Hammerton, Amalga-mated Press.

War in Pictures, The, Odhams Press Limited, six hb volumes.

World's Worst Disasters of the Twentieth Century, The, Octo-pus Books Limited, 1984.

Note: Many of these books can be found in second-hand bookshops. With some of the larger stores, for example, those in Hay-on-Wye (addresses in Yellow Pages), it would be worth writing to enquire if they have them and if they can be supplied by post.

Museums

Battle of Britain Memorial Flight, nr Sleaford, Lincolnshire.

Cabinet War Rooms, King Charles St, London SW1.

Cobbaton Combat Museum, Umberleigh, North Devon.

East Kent Maritime Museum, Royal Harbour, Ramsgate, Kent.

Eden Camp, nr Malton, North Yorkshire.

The Fleet Air Arm Museum, Yeovilton, nr Yeovil, Somerset.

Gloucester Folk Museum and Regimental Museum, Gloucester.

Imperial War Museum, Lambeth Road, London SE1.

Military Museum, Dorchester, Dorset.

Museum of Army Flying, Middle Wallop, Hants.

Museum of British Military Uniforms, Sleaford, Lincolnshire.

National Army Museum, Royal Hospital Road, London SW3.

Roman Army Museum, nr Haltwhistle, Northumberland.

Royal Air Force Museum, Grahame Park Way, Hendon, London NW9.

Royal Navy Submarine Museum, Gosport, Hants.

Southampton Hall of Aviation, Albert Road South, Southamp-ton.

Southsea Castle D-Day Museum, Southsea, Hants.
Ypres Tower Museum, Gun Garden, Rye, East Sussex.

Note: This is only a sample selection of the many war and military museums around the country.

Other

Action Videos, Iris Publishing Ltd, Kings Cliffe, Peterborough,
 PE8 6YH.
Mass-Observation Archive, Sussex University.
Pathe News Year To Remember Videos, Iris Publishing Ltd,
 Kings Cliffe, Peterborough, PE8 6YH.

9

TRAVEL AND COMMUNICATION

Time and motion

The time period of any novel has a direct relevance on the length of time your characters take to move about from one place to another. Stone Age people rarely moved from their cooking fires except to find food, and when they did travel, they went on foot. Hunting trips could therefore take a considerable time.

Through the centuries more elaborate means of travel evolved, and by the innovative Victorian era an impressive array of carriages and vehicles had emerged. And by the end of the twentieth century we can be whisked to New York in three hours on Concorde, yet spend endless frustrating hours waiting for an average flight to Europe, totally dependent on the various air traffic-control systems . . .

Even more awesome to those early cave-dwellers would be the fact that man has gone into space and stepped on to the moon . . . If he had ever known the words 'science fiction' in those far-off days, he would surely have described it thus.

But whether your fictional characters travel by bicycle, by train, in a romantic Russian troika or by interplanetary space-ship, it's essential to get the name and description of the vehicle right for the period, and not to let your characters arrive at their destinations in less time than is humanly possible.

This obvious fact was brought home to me in one of my early novels, when I sent my Victorian characters from Norfolk to the South Coast on horseback. In the travelling time I allowed them, the poor animals would probably have been dead from exhaustion long before they reached Brighton. It was a reader of the published novel who pointed this out. Neither I nor my editor had spotted the mistake, but it irked me for a long time afterwards.

This is one of the problems confronting the author who is sending characters on journeys. Class, too, is an unavoidable factor in your characters' movements. The farther back a historical novel is set, the less likelihood there is for working-class characters to move far from their own environment, while the better off would find ways and means to do so.

Until comparatively recently, whole working-class communities lived their entire lives without moving more than a few miles from the house or cottage where they were born. Neighbours were their extended family, and newcomers to an area were always regarded with suspicion.

It's also fair to say that people living in towns only a few miles outside London were mostly unaware of what their sovereign looked like. Until the advent of newspapers and journals, photography and television, royalty was able to preserve the kind of mystique and anonymity that it must often crave today.

But although the rich, and the adventurous, have always travelled, it was Queen Victoria who began to make travel fashionable, and she became the royal who was 'accessible' to the general public. It followed that the Grand Tour, generally encompassing India and/or Europe, became the desirable thing to do. And many an accompanying 'lady's companion' or children's governess discovered how narrow and cloistered life had been until then.

Roads and railways

How well do you remember the way your own town looked ten, or even five years ago? We have a splendid new road bridge over the railway in our busy seaside town. It has been there about a year, and the way the road layout looked before its time-saving convenience is already fading in my memory. So even if you are writing about your own area, or one that you think you know particularly well, you need to check that the roads you mention existed at that time.

Apart from choosing with care the actual road locations that you use in your novel, remember that their surfaces in days gone by could be a great hazard to the traveller. Simply getting from one place to another could take a huge amount of time, which is why few of our forefathers moved far from their own vicinity, especially after dark.

It was not so very long ago that many roads were ill lit, if lit at all, especially in country areas. There were no motorways or main roads, and in many places there were just dirt tracks linking towns and villages.

The dangers of travel were many, from that of organised highwaymen to the simple perils of rutted surfaces to trip and injure an unwary traveller, who would be unlikely to be found until daylight. There would be wild animals in the countryside, and all the unseen traps that darkness brings with it.

Finding out when cobblestones were replaced with firmer surfaces, or have just been left alone for their heritage value, is one of the things the historical novelist needs to know. In places like the York Castle Museum and Flambards in Cornwall, the reconstructed Victorian streets will give you an excellent scenario of streets and lighting as well as the shops and occupations of those times.

Railway travel became popular long before the car. As well

as the major railways, there were many small, private railways. I have a small paperback called *The Story of Cornwall's Railways*, which is one of the set of 'holiday' paperbacks I've collected, and which has proved endlessly useful for my Cornish-based novels. The amount of detail and research information packed into these small booklets is quite amazing.

The advent of the railways opened up much of Britain that was hitherto completely unknown to its people. It's hard for us to comprehend now how thrilling were those organised works 'outings' that took people by bus, tram or train to places perhaps only twenty miles away. Those places could be as new and exciting as foreign countries are today.

Such is the British passion for railways that railway books can be found everywhere, from platform bookshops to second-hand bookshops. Larger volumes that should be found in libraries include *Railway Reflections*, a collection of pictures from the pre-war railway years. It covers extensive regions of Britain and has background information about each picture.

Jowett's Railway Atlas of Great Britain and Ireland gives a detailed record of the railways in existence in Great Britain and Ireland during the first two decades of the twentieth century. It includes all additions up to the mid-1980s.

The Guinness Railway Book covers the history, development and records of the world's railway systems, including the work of the greatest railway engineers. I cannot leave out a further book about my own favourite great engineer. *Isambard Kingdom Brunel* tells of his pioneering achievements in railway engineering, bridge-building and ship-building, and has been a useful source of research on numerous occasions.

There are many museums devoted to railway and other travel memorabilia. These, and the various suggested places to visit that are mentioned in this and other chapters, form only a fraction of the many sites where research can be carried out.

Of interest to historical novelists, for instance, might be the Isle of Wight Steam Railway, where passengers actually use the old wooden railway carriages on part of the track once used by Queen Victoria on her way to Osborne House.

Vehicles old and new

Motor museums are one of the most enjoyable ways of 'doing research' on old cars. Here you can see exactly the kinds of early motor vehicles in use, smell the leather, and see the exquisite workmanship with which some of those vehicles were put together.

For the purist, there is usually plenty of detail on the date of manufacture, fuel consumption, engine maker and so on. One of the most well known of these museums is at Beaulieu in the New Forest. Vintage cars form only a small part of the exhibits on show, and this theme is repeated in other motor museums around the country, some of which are listed below.

I seem to have collected a number of small books on vehicles over the years. My copy of *The Observer's Book of Automobiles* was published in 1968, and goes into great illustrated detail about the early days of cars and those manufactured up until that date. I've no doubt there are later editions of the book.

Veterans and Vintage Cars would save you the trouble of visiting museums, and give you the comfort of doing your research from your armchair. It is highly illustrated, with a lot of background information on the vehicles and their prices. It also has snippets about the people who used them, including a splendid photograph of King Edward VII when Prince of Wales, in a twelve-horsepower Daimler in 1899.

Another fascinating bit of nostalgia in this book is the

inclusion of two motoring summonses in 1896. The poor unfortunate was required to appear in court in Bow Street for exceeding the two-miles-an-hour speed limit, and for neglecting to have a footman preceding him. Now there's food for a novelist's thought!

Two paperback booklets that have proved useful come in a series called Shire Albums. One is called *Austerity Motoring 1939–1950*, and the other is *The Country Garage*, both of which cover what their names imply. There are many other booklets in this series, such as *Old Trams* and *Traction Engines*.

And speaking of traction engines, an excellent book with full colour illustrations is *Steam Traction Engines, Wagons and Rollers*. This is also part of a hardback series of books, and as so often happens, the bibliography yields a further source of research reading. Included in it are the following: *Lorries, Trucks and Van 1897–1927*; *Trams in Colour since 1945*; *The Pocket Encyclopaedia of Buses and Trolleybuses before 1919* and its sequel, covering the years from 1919 to 1945.

Going back to older times, a small paperback I've sometimes referred to is *Through Cornwall by Coach, 1795*, which is subtitled 'Impressions of the Old Duchy', and is written in diary form of a gentleman's leisurely journey through the county. At this time, the lumbering old stage waggons (his spelling), drawn by eight horses, took three weeks to reach London from Cornwall, while stage coaches could travel between Truro and Torpoint in a day! Although his book gives little more in the way of vehicle information, it has some fascinating details on the author's actual journey, and the prices he was charged for accommodation and food. A second book written in the same style, is dated 1885.

Another useful small paperback is called *Discovering Carts and Wagons*, which details the country vehicles in use in various counties of England and Wales, and with a glossary of terms relevant to the construction of the vehicles.

A useful reference guide as to the dates when the various modes of transport come into being can be found in the *Shell Book of Firsts*, mentioned earlier in this book. Among other items, it gives such details as to when the first petrol-driven motor car was built (1883); who was the first doctor to use a motor car (Dr Carlos C. Booth of Ohio, in 1895); and the date of the first motor-car radio in use (1922).

A considerable section of the book is devoted to motoring, with many interesting little facts and anecdotes that could be incorporated or adapted so authentically in fiction: an example would be the first motoring fatality, way back in 1896, when a lady was run over and had her skull fractured by the wheel of a car.

Feminist tendencies were in evidence very early on in the history of motoring. Bertha Benz took her husband's car out without his knowledge and went driving with her sons in 1888, enjoying the freedom of German roads. The enterprising Frau Benz was obliged to make several running repairs during the drive, unblocking the carburettor with a hatpin and later insulating a short-circuited ignition wire with her garter. There's plenty of food for thought there for the novelist, and far more to this useful reference book than mere dates and 'firsts'.

Many other reference guides provide basic facts. Such guides may only give you the bare bones, but will inevitably lead you on to further research sources. One of these is Hutchinson's *Factfinder*, which gives you facts, figures, dates and events. The Thomas Cook Archive and Library provides another excellent research facility, and a query letter will usually produce whatever travel detail you require.

However far and wide you go for your researches, in my opinion at least one comprehensive overall book dealing with facts and figures is an essential addition to a novelist's book shelf. And, very often, you realise you need little more than a few accurate facts to make a scene come to life.

Filling your novel with masses of research material that you have laboriously found and which does nothing to add to the story of your characters is the mark of the amateur. Filtering the necessary and important facts in between the lines of your fictional events gives them authenticity and believability, and is the professional way.

Sea and shipping

One of the problems that many novelists face is finding out how long sailing ships took to cross the Atlantic, or the routes that they voyaged to reach Australia or even somewhere as relevatively near as the Mediterranean countries. It's one thing to send your characters off on a long sea voyage, but quite another to know whether or not it's still spring when they arrive, or if the seasons have turned upside down, and whether what was summer when they left is still summer when they arrive!

There are many books on navigation and old sea routes, as well as detailed autobiographies of sailors past and present, who will have charted their routes in minute detail. Any good librarian will suggest suitable books for whatever you require. Some will become involved in your project and look it up for you, but don't count on that!

I've found The Seafarers Series in Time-Life Books very useful. If you visit any of the many maritime museums around the country, try to enlist the aid of the curator. People are always willing to help, especially if they know you're writing a novel. Again, the children's library, with its books of facts and figues, may be a useful source.

Air travel

Overlapping slightly with the section on the Second World War in the previous chapter, *Women in Airforce Blue* gives the story of the Women's Royal Air Force from 1918 until the present day, and is an invaluable source of information on a woman's role in the service, written by an expert.

Great Moments in Aviation gives you exactly what it says, and includes 30 illustrated accounts of great moments in aviation history. If you want to know about the great balloon escape from Paris in 1870, or details of the most famous round-the-world flights, all retold by knowledgeable writers on their subject, this is for you. Following on more dramatic lines is *Drama in the Air*, a collection of highly tense, true stories that may well make you decide to keep your feet on the ground in future, but which can also provide you with plenty of ideas for your fictional characters to deal with.

Interesting general backgrounds are provided in several pocket guides. *abc Airport Operations* gives you all the information you need on 'behind the scenes' activities of what goes on at an international airport. And *abc European Airports* gives you details of all the well-known airports, including maps, services and facilities. *Airliners*, subtitled 'The flagships of the jet age', is a comprehensive guide to all the jet planes of the century, including a pictorial record of the planes and insignias of many different countries.

When travelling by air, it's also a good idea to arm yourself with a notebook for the inevitable long wait at the airport. You can spend the time usefully doing on-the-spot research for background information, colour, and the *modus operandi* of the personnel . . . this can continue when you're on board the plane as well. Keeping a diary-type record of any journey that you make is a good idea.

If you want to see how it feels to sit in Concorde without

going to the expense of buying the ticket, there are various places that provide you with the experience while still staying on the ground. The Fleet Air Arm Museum at Yeovilton in Somerset is one of them. As well as seeing the size, shape and incredible flimsiness of First World War planes, you can visit the cockpit of Concorde and walk through the aircraft while never leaving the ground.

I've been to many different countries and collected a mountain of leaflets and guidebooks from museums and other exhibits, including the Smithsonian Air and Space Museum in Washington DC. Yet the International Helicopter Museum is right here in the town where I live. One of these days I mean to visit it, and this is another example of missing what's right under your nose. But as yet, I've never wanted to put my characters into a helicopter ...

Air travel has gone far beyond those early tentative days we all laugh about in those black-and-white silent movies. Now there's space travel ...

Space travel

For an accurate look at man's first flight to the moon, *From the Flightdeck: Apollo 11* will give you all the details of the flight mission, including actual NASA voice transcripts, diagrams and photographs. And *Aerospace Chronology* is a source of reference into the history of aviation history.

If you're travelling in the States, then a visit to the Kennedy Space Centre in Florida can be an awesome experience. On the lawns as you enter, the rockets are on display like giant fireworks, but everything gets more and more technical as you go through the museum areas. There are short films describing the work that they do there, and finally you can go on a bus trip around the site. The building housing the huge space rockets is so vast it belies your own vision. The United States flag in one top corner of the building is the size of several football pitches.

If you're lucky enough to be in the area at the right time, there are viewing areas nearby where you can observe one of the fairly frequent rocket launches. Space travel is brought down to earth for the visitors' benefit, but it only makes you more incredulous of the gruelling training and bravery of the astronauts who fly into space, and the huge achievements of the people who made it possible.

Communications – by post and telephone

Down to earth again, and the more mundane ways of communication. It's easy enough nowadays to pick up a telephone, send a fascimile message or write a letter, knowing that it will reach its destination in a reasonable time. Even if the person at the other end of the telephone isn't in, there may well be an answering machine to record a message for him. Life is very convenient for us.

Imagine then a time when the only way to send a letter to the other side of the world was by one of the sailing ships going to the new colonies of America or Australia. In many cases it was unlikely they would ever reach their destination, and if they did, the information in the letters would be long out of date, and the recipients may well have moved on, or even died.

In 1794 the Penny Post Office arrived on the scene, and an article in *The Times* of 28 February that year reported that there would be six deliveries a day in all parts of London. It advises readers that 'persons posting letters by nine a.m., at the distance of ten miles from the Penny Post Office, may receive answers from London the same day'. Some things have not improved for the better. (*How They Lived*, Asa Briggs, Volume 111, 1700–1815.)

Air mail was to come much later and was an unimagined method of communication until this century, pioneered by the daring flying men after the First World War with their private air services. Newspapers provided much of the news that people received. In the far corners of the country, little would be known of London society except what was written in the newspapers of the day. And few poorer people would have read them, or in many cases, been able to read. So even a scant knowledge of cities, high society and foreign countries would not come within their horizons at all. This is a useful thing to remember when you want to move your fictional characters out of their normal country environment into the big bad city. Or, conversely, when you place your city characters into what would seem to them to be an unbelievable backwater.

Sources relevant to this chapter

Books (pub. dates given where known)

abc Airport Operations, Robert Palmer, Ian Allan, 1989.
abc European Airports, Alan Wright, Ian Allan, 1989.
Aerospace Chronology, Michael Taylor, Tri-Service Press, 1989.
Airliners, Bill Gunston, Treasure Press, 1981.
Austerity Motoring 1939–1950, Shire Publications, 1987.
Canals in Colour, Anthony Burton, Blandford Press, 1974.
Country Garage, The, Lyn E. Morris, Shire Publications, 1985.
Cruise-Ships of the World, William H. Miller, Patrick Stephens, 1989.

10

GEOGRAPHY, PAST AND PRESENT

Using maps and gazetteers

Using maps to plot your characters' journeys is one of the simplest ways of doing geographical research. You merely have to follow the roads and railway lines on the map to get your characters from A to Z and back again ... When I'm writing a novel, I often create my own sketch maps for an area, whether it's real or imaginary. Actually setting this down on paper gives me a sense of reality for my setting.

But it always surprises me when new authors say they know nothing about the geography of a place, so they couldn't possibly write about it. There is so much accessible information about our world nowadays that there's no excuse for an author getting it wrong, as Thomas Hardy did over Brazil. Most local newsagents have a mass of maps and gazetteers on their shelves.

No matter in what location you set your book, it will be advantageous, if not essential, to know something about the terrain, the climate, agriculture, industry and possibly tourist accessibility. You can discover all that from maps. I still have my old school atlas, which I've often referred to for certain facts. In the intervening years, contemporary industry may have changed, but the climate and terrain will be constant. Such an atlas is a good example of a children's book that simplifies and explains in great detail.

Pears Cyclopaedia always includes an excellent gazetteer, and is an endlessly comprehensive research volume for the novelist. You can find out the essential points of a town or city at a glance in the gazetteer section. A random look at my old 1965 copy (shortly to be renewed) tells me that Cape Town was the capital of Cape Hope Province; it's situated in Table Bay, 30 miles north of the Cape of Good Hope; there is direct rail communication with Rhodesia, Transvaal, Orange and Natal; it has docks and a cathedral; it exports wool, gold and diamonds. It also gives the population numbers for the year 1960. Obviously, this would only scratch the surface for a novel set in South Africa in the sixties, but it would be a good start.

I've never said that you *have* to visit a place to absorb the ambience, to walk the streets, and talk at length with the local people in order to write a believable novel. I also suspect that the published authors who pompously insist on this to beginners may put them off for good. If you *can* visit a place, and you wish to do so, it's your choice. If you can't, then find other ways of researching it.

Of course it would be a help, if, for instance, your book were set in a contemporary big city's backstreets, to hang around at midnight, observing the junkies and the sleazier parts of city life ... but I wouldn't recommend it. There are enough documentaries in books and on the screen to give anyone enough background colour for that.

But to find out the exact locations of the streets I needed in a novel, then an A–Z of a locality would be useful. Writing to the publicity departments of any large town council will usually result in a mass of information, local maps and the like. Some of this may cost you money, but much of it will be in the form of free handouts, especially if the town in question is on the tourist route. Sending a preliminary letter with a SAE, or making a telephone call, to the local tourist information office will clarify.

For Regency novelists, or others using the same era, the *A to Z of Regency London* can be found in the Guildhall Library, Aldermanbury. This contains Horwood's maps, first printed from 1799 to 1819.

Many novelists prefer to invent towns, islands, streets and even imaginary countries. The science-fiction author invariably does so. There's absolutely no reason why you shouldn't do this, but if you *do* use real locations, always check that places are where you say they are. There's nothing so maddening for a reader than to read a novel set in her own home town, and to find that the author has set down, say, a fictional cinema in the area of the local churchyard . . . though five hundred years ago, there may well have been an ancient burial ground where the cinema is now . . . You see why you need to check.

It's easy enough to keep your main locations authentic but vague enough to cover a wide area, and to invent a house or business being carried on there. For instance, you could say that your fictional lawyer's chambers were in a prosperous part of Edinburgh, and that your nervous female character was overawed by the brass nameplate on the door telling her that here were the chambers of Messrs Macduff, Brodie, Macdonald and Macdonald. Such information would be adequate to imply all that the reader needed to know. It all depends on the importance of your scene, and the way you depict the characters.

Ordnance survey maps and county magazines

For absolute historical accuracy, then old ordnance survey maps are your best guides. These usually cover specific and quite localised areas of the country, and show places in great detail, naming old farms and spinneys and manor houses, and often providing you with rural names you hadn't thought of, or even heard of, but which will add colour to your novel.

You can buy individual ordnance survey maps covering all parts of the British Isles. Sunday newspapers often advertise them, or a reputable shop such as W. H. Smith will find details for you and order them. For the dedicated researcher, there is also a publication called *The Ordnance Survey Atlas of Great Britain*, but for the average novelist who wants to write about one small area with authenticity, this would probably be an unnecessary expense. A modern edition of the reprinted David & Charles first edition can be obtained from HMSO, London or Southampton.

You do need to evaluate the time and money you're prepared to spend on research. To me, it seems like sheer lunacy to spend days poring over an ordnance survey map to find out if a right of way existed in some remote rural area in mediaeval times, for instance, when the author's leeway can perfectly well allow you to invent such a thing for the purposes of your Victorian or contemporary novel.

A novel is, in the end, a work of fiction, and while you would hardly be so foolish as to set down the Coliseum in the middle of France, there are limits as to how far you go with your research. So be realistic about it, and know when to call a halt on all the delving and diving and get on with the real work of writing your book.

Magazines of local county interest are to be found everywhere, and can give a comprehensive idea of the general interests of each county. County magazines can give you fascinating detail into ancient local customs and events, and also give you the correct terminology for each area. A dap in Somerset is quite different from a dap in Yorkshire, for instance. It's worth buying up a number of issues of a particular county magazine for the area you are writing about, to get the 'feel' of it.

A good place to find back numbers of such magazines seems to be in doctors' or dentists' waiting-rooms. You could always beg or borrow one or two from your obliging dentist or GP . . . especially if you offer to bring a pile of other magazines in exchange. They have to get their patients' reading material from somewhere.

As well as buying or borrowing county magazines in any large newsagent's, a set of volumes called the *Victoria County History* is held in many libraries. Your library may only hold the editions pertinent to your county and the surrounding ones, but main county-town libraries may hold them all. The volumes contain a mass of detailed information, with maps, plans and statistics.

Fodor's and other guides

When researching foreign countries for my novels, I have found *Fodor's* and similar guides of immense use. Libraries stock them, and they are obviously on general sale, but all the ones I own I've bought from library sales. I've collected a number of them now, even those I didn't envisage using immediately as novel backgrounds, simply because they were sold off so cheaply and are such good value.

Among my non-used ones I have *Fodor's Japan and East Asia*, and *Fodor's South America*. Among my well-used ones are *Fodor's Greece* and *Fodor's Tunisia*. If you haven't yet discovered this type of guide, I thoroughly recommend them. And if you think they just contain current tourist information, then think again.

Included in the excellent amount of information in my *Fodor's Tunisia* book, for instance, are details about the landscape, climate, vegetation, social and political systems, language and education. You will find details of up-to-date travel and best time to go, and getting around the country, as well as the usual tourist information such as shopping areas, sporting facilities, museums and so on.

But there's also far more that can be of use to the novelist. These guides go into the history and culture of each country. You learn about the food and drink, the arts and crafts, and you have a glossary of useful words and phrases. There are town maps and a pull-out map, and the books are also illustrated. I've incorporated a lot of information from *Fodor's Tunisia* (and others) for two of my novels, and have been applauded for my fascinating and accurate detail, yet I've never been to Tunisia.

Berlitz travel guides are pocket books that are mainly intended for tourists, but don't ignore their potential for research purposes. If you know little of the pertinent language of your foreign setting, they can give you useful phrases for your characters to say, albeit in a rather limited way! Don't expect to find love scenes detailed in a guide book, but if you want your touring Brit to ask the way to the railway station or how to ask for something for an upset stomach at the chemist, then this is the answer.

Foreign phrase books and dictionaries are other useful references regarding language. You can get stuck on something as simple as days of the week, or clothing sizes, or currency, and a phrase book won't cost the earth.

A few years ago I enrolled in a Spanish language class and became so absorbed in it that I eventually (amazingly) got a GCSE grade A in Spanish. The teacher was Spanish, and was very keen on giving us background and historical information about the country. The textbooks she used complemented this idea. She also brought her own guide books and films to the class, which added to the interest in Spain.

For me, it did far more. It resulted in my writing various

novels with Spanish backgrounds, which meant I could also offset the cost of the classes against income tax.

Travel brochures

Obviously it's not always possible to travel for background information, especially if your novel is going to cover a wide canvas, perhaps jumping from one international location to the next. So you need to be accurate with distances and any global time changes, and one of the simplest ways of doing this is simply to consult a map. Most of them give all the relevant information you need.

Travel agents sometimes supply maps and other travel details free, and not just from their high-street offices. I've been to various 'travel evenings' arranged by local travel agents at which they give away maps and other information supplied by the travel firms.

One of these events that I went to provided typical food of the region to try and to tempt tourists into booking a holiday. (A bonus to the whole evening was receiving first prize in the raffle – a bottle of regional wine.) You are usually shown films of the area as well. If such a travel evening covering a location you may want to write about is advertised, take advantage of an interesting evening out, and collect your free research material at the same time.

The glossy brochures that you see in the windows of travel agents are meant to be a tempter to foreign and exotic places. The photographs inside are just as enticing, and an amazing amount of information can be gleaned from them if you take the trouble to look beyond the mere holiday trappings and see the location as a plot possibility.

I always maintain that research and plotting go together. One opens up new possibilities for the other. Small items I might discover in the course of 'doing the research' can produce an entire change of storyline, or result in a significant scene that makes all the difference to the strength or downfall of a character. This is what I consider the real magic of research, because once you begin, you never know just what you're going to turn up.

But back to the travel brochures . . . and why not stay with Tunisia for a moment? In one of my brochures a typical scene in a souk is pictured. It's one of the delightful and fragrant marketplaces, teeming with people, and with goods of every description on display outside the small dark shops. Overhead the sky is dazzlingly blue, and people are smiling and happy. A young girl is examining a hammered brass object in a huge display while a gnarled Tunisian is explaining its significance, or encouraging her to buy . . .

It's a simple scene, meant to entice us to book up a sunshine holiday immediately. But look at it again, this time with a researcher's eyes. Has the heroine discovered something exciting amongst the trash? Did she go there intending to look for some treasure? Is she an undercover agent looking for drugs? Is this an arranged coded meeting with the old brass seller? Is the crowd closing in on her for some reason? Is the sinister man nearby about to stab her? Or will he kill the brass seller to stop him revealing the whereabouts of the next clue on the trail of . . .? Is she an heiress about to be abducted in the midst of a busy crowd? Has she been reckless in shopping alone in a foreign city, and about to have all her money stolen?

All these imaginary situations are there for the taking from one small picture in a travel brochure. Just open your mind and ask yourself the basic questions of how, why, what if, etc.

Since travel agents offer these brochures free, arm yourself with a few and you'll be surprised at how much useful information they contain. Nobody wants to be accused of writing a travelogue instead of a novel, so beware of packing too much detail into your book. But whether you want to let your characters visit the main attractions of a city, or be determined to avoid them and head off the beaten track, I guarantee you'll find something in a brochure to add to your other researches.

You don't even have to move far from your armchair to obtain brochures. Newspapers and magazines advertise them widely, and you can send or telephone for them. A travel agent may also send you a brochure of your choice. And TV travel programmes are endlessly popular, so there's hardly any reason for us not to know about foreign locations any more.

For an entertaining and delightful look into Victorian travelling, *With Passport and Parasol* was published in 1989 by BBC Books in conjunction with a Radio 4 series. It tells of the adventurous travels of seven Victorian ladies of differing status, told from their diaries and autobiographies. Since these ladies include a journalist, a mystic and a society hostess, the revelations are varied and full of insights.

Foreign locations

If you're lucky enough to travel widely, then collecting the relevant brochures from any town or interesting location that you visit is an obvious must. If you're an armchair traveller, then turn again to the travel brochures. In many of them, you will find addresses to write to for more detailed information on a particular location.

This doesn't apply only to addresses in holiday brochures advertising foreign locations. Several years ago, my husband and I took a driving holiday covering Washington State, Oregon and California. We already had a USA map from previous visits, and on the back of this map is a list of names, addresses and telephone numbers of all the State Travel Offices in the USA.

Assuming we would get more relevant information by applying direct, my husband telephoned the three states mentioned above, requesting maps and any tourist and accommodation information available. Within days, we received three huge packages of maps, brochures and tourist books, sent free by air mail – and all supplying marvellous background material for future novels. If you travel to the USA, you can pick up all this kind of material at any information kiosk.

I've found it interesting, while travelling, to buy foreign magazines and newspapers. Obviously these are most useful if they're printed in English, unless you have a smattering of the language. But even without these aids, you can glean a reasonable idea of the countryside, fashions, food and general interests from the illustrations and advertisements.

Also, most foreign countries have consulates in this country. It might be worth a letter with SAE requesting any specific information you require.

Collecting holiday and other ephemera

Combining business with pleasure by collecting holiday and other ephemera is one of my favourite parts of a holiday. I have never returned from any holiday without bringing back something that may be of use in a novel, whether it's theatre tickets, programmes or brochures of places visited. Also, I always buy postcards of each place I visit.

Taking photographs is a must, but they may not always come out as you wish, so a professional picture on a postcard with a brief scrap of information on the back can be enough to trigger your memory. It's so easy to forget, and a visual reminder conjures up pictures in the mind quicker than anything else.

When I stay in hotels, I admit to collecting the soaps and shampoos they provide. As well as being reminders of some great (or not so great) holidays, I may want to put my characters there in some future book, and I like to know how well each hotel catered for its guests. I collect sugars from airlines and restaurants, and while these trivial items may never be used in a book, they too, sharpen my memory of my travels, as do my plane tickets, and all details of booking.

I've bought jigsaws of San Francisco, and framed pictures of the New York skyline. I have a pictorial calendar of Niagara Falls and another of Victoria, Australia. Both calendars are out of date now, but the pictorial data has appeared in my novels.

I have a bronze statue of Aphrodite from Cyprus and a little fool's-gold statue of a miner from California. Nearer to home, I have a slate coal-mining model from Wales, and my Innes family crest from Scotland, as well as pieces of Cornish serpentine and a ghastly photo of my husband and myself in Holland, dressed in 'authentic' Dutch costume.

None of this is vital to research in writing a novel. But I think that anything that reminds you vividly of a place when you write about it, is worth its salt. If you're *going* there, why not bring back something to make your trip memorable?

And if you're not going to a place yourself, then maybe your friends or family are. They can usually be persuaded to pick up one or two of any useful brochures or leaflets they collect from their visits to chateaux in France or vineyards in Spain. Or even a trip on the North Yorkshire railway . . .

It doesn't take up much space in anyone's luggage to bring home two items instead of one. If you're willing to pay for extra guidebooks from anywhere especially interesting, cajole them into bringing those back too.

Don't forget anniversaries when you think about collecting

research ephemera. I don't mean the usual holiday times, such as Easter and Christmas, but the social and worldwide anniversaries that always produce a crop of articles in the tabloid newspapers and magazines. Ascot Week, the Henley Royal Regatta, D-Day and Wimbledon fortnight are cases in point. It was in one of the tabloid magazines that I read an excellent article on past Wimbledons which showed the changing style of women's tennis dress. It also told me that ladies never served overarm until 1937, and that the all-white rule began as early as the 1890s, to avoid displaying perspiration stains. Now those were a couple of gems . . .

Photography

I've only briefly mentioned the most important thing of all in my holiday equipment. As well as taking notebook and pens and keeping a diary account of everywhere I go, I never travel without my camera.

My husband also brings his video camera, and obviously this is marvellous for recording any sound and visual happening, such as Morris dancing in Dorset or an Italian wedding that we once saw in Assisi. (I was sure it had Mafia overtones . . .)

But to use the video information in your researches, you then have to set it all up on the TV screen, and take notes. In the end, I think it's more useful for research purposes to take plenty of still photographs.

And I do mean plenty. It's certainly not overdoing it to photograph street scenes, markets, beaches, sunsets, airports, the interior of your aeroplane, churches, your motel room, apartment or hotel. Just as the picture in the holiday brochure can reveal more than you first thought, you often find that you've captured more on film than you intended. In one picture

I could never be absolutely sure, but it looked very much like a pickpocket at work in one of the crowded street scenes I photographed abroad.

Just as you should allow your research to speak to you, by being receptive to everything it has to offer to enhance your work, so you should make your photos work for you. If they inspire you into writing a new scene or inventing a new character to include in your novel, then the price of the film will have been worthwhile.

The chiropractor who fixed my back in Florida didn't mind me photographing him, or the equipment in his offices that I'd never seen before. The lovely doorman at our hotel in New Orleans, dressed in his beige uniform of safari jacket, shorts and pith helmet, didn't mind either.

I wonder if I would have remembered either of these people or events quite so clearly without my photos to remind me. And while you can get all the pictures you require from books, magazines and brochures, it's far more memorable to take them yourself, if you can.

Photographs showing people in their own environment or working on their particular craft, can really enliven your writing when you set them beside you as you write. You'll remember the heat of the day as you watched the women working in the Spanish fields. You'll recall how you shivered slightly in the cool musty wine cellars of France. You'll remember the smiles of the girls doing their traditional dances under the stars for the tourists.

You'll remember all this more clearly if you took your own photographs, because for those brief moments, you were involved in their various activities. You, the camera and your subject were an invincible threesome. Refer to Chapter 1 regarding dating and labelling your pictures.

Sources relevant to this chapter

Books

A to Z of Regency London, Guildhall Library, Aldermanbury.
Berlitz Travel Guides.
Collins Phrase Books
Fodor's Guide Books
Ordnance Survey Atlas of Great Britain, The, reprinted first edition, early 1800s, David & Charles, Newton Abbott, Devon.
Ordnance Survey Atlas of Great Britain, The, modern edition, HMSO, London & Southampton.
Penguin Atlas of World History.
Times Concise Atlas, The.
Times Illustrated Road Atlas, The.
Victoria County History (libraries).
With Passport and Parasol, BBC Books, 1989.
World Gazetteer, Chambers.

Other

County magazines.
Tourist offices.
Travel brochures.

11

USING THE RESEARCH - A WORKED EXAMPLE

Finding out the facts for *The Bannister Girls*

When I decided to write a book set during the First World War, it was a complete departure for me. Until then, I had written many historical novels set in the eighteenth and nineteenth centuries, a number of contemporary romances, and some teenage novels.

I generally like to choose my background first, with my characters and plot being very dependent on the background/setting. I knew very little about the First World War, other than the basic facts that most people glean during a lifetime. So where to begin, and why did I choose this particular background?

Firstly, I like the drama and emotions that a war brings out in people. We all show our best and worst faces in times of great stress, and never more than in wartime. As well as the high drama on a broad scale, there are also many trivial, but no less pertinent details on a domestic scale.

Secondly, it was a period in the near past which I was becoming increasingly interested in writing about. I had 'done' what is considered 'real' historicals (though I still write them, and enjoy them immensely), and the contemporary scene no longer held quite as much interest for me as a writer as the lure of nostalgia.

The Bannister Girls eventually became the first book in my change of direction. The title refers to the three daughters of a wealthy family, and here I must say that having no more than the *idea* of using the First World War as background, I then decided on my characters.

The next idea was to make them contrasting characters, and to further the credibility of this, it seemed a good idea to make their parents unlikely partners. Such parents could easily produce differing traits in their children – especially those who conformed, and those who did not.

So Sir Fred Bannister was a self-made, slightly vulgar and red-blooded man in the wool trade. Lady Clemence was an outright snob, whose autocratic stiffness was slightly based on the regal bearing of Queen Mary. Lady Clemence's main aim in life was for her daughters to make good marriages.

So far, so good, and there was no special research needed to invent such characters. Nor did I need anything other than my imagination to create my central character, Angel. She was the youngest and prettiest daughter, still starry-eyed at the thought of romance. Ellen was the questioning and rebellious one, enthralled by the suffragette movement, and Louise was compliant, married, and very much her mother's daughter.

The publisher's blurb describes the book thus:

The twentieth century was a decade and a half old at the outbreak of the Great War, but little had altered since the days of Queen Victoria. All women, regardless of their status, had well defined roles in life – a life whose strict boundaries were rarely over-stepped. But the advent of war, which stole the lives of a generation of young men, slowly began to erode such man-made barriers to equality and fulfilment.

The Bannister Girls is a poignant novel of love and war, and the rites of passage of a generation that will mould the Britain of the new century. Will the mêlée of death and despair that is the Great War prove or destroy the strength of its sons and daughters . . .?

This sums up my intentions very well. I wanted to show, during the time span of the novel, how the lives of people were changed forever because of a war. In this case, my characters weren't three 'ordinary' girls, but those that the war hadn't yet touched, and because of their privileged background, possibly never would. But that wouldn't have made a story . . .

The outline

Not everyone plans a novel in detail before they start. Some people begin with a character or an idea, then start writing, and see where it leads them. This can work perfectly well. For a longer novel, such as a saga, I think a certain amount of planning is essential. Otherwise, it's like jumping on a train without knowing where you're going. Fun, perhaps, but a bit aimless, and certainly a possible waste of a journey.

The first thing I did for *The Bannister Girls* was to decide on the time span of the book. I chose not to begin with pre-war days, or the very beginning of the war, since the drama of that time wasn't going to affect the metamorphosis of my characters. I wanted them to be almost lulled into a false sense of sameness, with nothing really happening to change their world except for the nuisance value of wartime.

So the year when the book begins is 1915, and it ends when the war ends. This, I felt, was also essential, to bring all the events in my books to a natural conclusion. Thus, I had a three-year span in which to balance scenes and action. From then on, I concocted my haphazard outline.

I use these words quite candidly. There is no mystique in the way in which I work. During the writing/researching period, my desk is a mish-mash of reference books, scribbled notes, maps, leaflets, lists of names and chronological data. The first rough outline may not bear much relation to the finished product, but is quite vital to me. It is my own guideline from the white-hot ideas in my mind, and is usually scribbled down with great speed and enthusiasm.

I don't research anything at this time. The outline is not meant to be a finished synopsis, just a reasonable working background. I know there will be much research to do later, and a more detailed synopsis to work out. Areas that will need thorough researching I always indicate by writing CHECK in capital letters alongside the suggested plot development.

This was the beginning of my first rough outline for *The Bannister Girls*:

Begin 1915. Three well-to-do sisters – London home. Father a Sir, but more rough and ready than his aristocratic wife. Angel is chief character. Names of others to decide. CHECK fashions, lifestyles.

Scene-setting for first chapter. Angel away from home for the night (reason?), must meet hero early on. Rainy night, both looking for a cab, he's French, in Royal Flying Corps.

CHECK RFC details. (Why would a Frenchman be in RFC?) Instant attraction between them, and they spend night together. (Is this feasible with 1915 morals?) Later she feels cheap and deserted.

Parents discover she hadn't been with girlfriend that night. Uproar. Because of this, and the war threats to the capital, Father moves family to country home in Somerset, though he'll also spend time in Yorkshire at his wool mills.

CHECK. (Sub-plot with father having mistress in York-shire?)

Hero Jacques de Ville's home in France - CHECK vineyards etc. - his father extremely wealthy. CHECK all details of planes, air battles etc. from Jacques' viewpoint. CHECK uniforms - RFC and others. CHECK slang etc.

Other subplots should involve Angel's sisters, also her girlfriend and family. One sister to become land-girl - CHECK details, uniform etc. (Married sister's husband killed?)

Find reason for Angel to go to France. Jacques missing in air-raid not enough for Angel to abandon home. Could she discover her father's infidelity? (Yes - I like this.) She would be shocked and hurt, desperate to get away. CHECK what she would do at the Front, having no skills.

CHECK locations in - London, Somerset, Yorkshire, France. CHECK communications, women's wartime occupations, wartime social activities. Book will end immediately after Armistice Day. CHECK details.

How much and how little to include

You can't fail to notice from the above how many questions I ask myself. There are always choices to be made. Research for a lengthy saga necessarily involves a lot of reading and note-taking, and in the end you may find you only use a small proportion of the facts you've discovered. You may also choose and discard many possibilities along the way, but nothing is wasted. The more you know about the period and background of your novel, the way that people lived and loved, worked and died, the more authentic your novel will become.

In a novel of this kind, the domestic details of family life have to be just as correct as the wider world details. But for the former, common sense will tell you many things. My first paragraph, below, was constructed from a mixture of many sources that needed no researching. Most of it came from my memory of films, television programmes and old magazines, together with the necessary imagination to create a visual scene.

The girls from the old pickle factory, now patriotically changed over to munitions, swore colourfully in the sudden downpour of rain glossing the streets as smoothly as sugar icing on a bun. Angel Bannister tried not to notice their jostling as she splashed along in her high-button boots, trying to avoid the puddles. The cold March wind had freshened, whipping against her cheeks and catching her breath.

A further paragraph on the first page:

The London streets were congested with people caught out by the storm, as horse-drawn traffic, trams and private motors all tried to converge into spaces seemingly too small for them.

None of this involved detailed research. It was enough to create the busy London scene and set the location and bad weather. The month of March, otherwise undated, could be reliably expected to have at least one stormy day.

But since my heroine was about to meet her hero, research was needed very early on in the book. I wanted to describe Jacques' distinctive Royal Flying Corps uniform for Angel's benefit, and for the reader's. I could have made him a soldier or sailor, but since these were the early days of daredevil flying, with all the danger and glamour attached to them, being a pilot would make him even more of a dashing figure to her.

To have left the description, however brief, out would have wasted the uniqueness of his profession. And it *was* brief - just Angel's observations of his breast badge, with the initial RFC held in the outstretched wings of a swift.

I had to search for details about the RFC and the craft they flew, but since Jacques was every bit as important to the story as Angel, I wanted to know all I could about him. My sources included *Reaching for the Skies* by Ivan Rendell, which had good photographs of the pilots and their aircraft; and *War in Three Dimensions* by Air Vice-Marshall E. J. Kingston-McCloughry, which a friend found for me in a sale for ten pence.

In this little book (and others) I discovered that the RAF was formed on 1 April 1918, incorporating the RFC - and I particularly noted down that fact. As Jacques would still be a serviceman at that time, it would be unrealistic to let the change pass without some reference to it. Such little points can make or break the credibility of the writing.

I must also acknowledge my avid reading of *A Killing for the Hawks*, a novel by Frederick E. Smith, whch gave me a marvellous insight into the men and machines of the Royal Flying Corps, told from the male author's viewpoint. The only other fiction I read was *Von Richthofen and Brown* which gave an account of the aviation life of the legendary Red Baron of Germany. These two novels brought the dogfights of the early days of air warfare vividly to life.

Blending facts with fiction

My main sources of research for *The Bannister Girls* were books. Apart from locations known to me in Somerset, London and Yorkshire, and the layout of Bristol Temple Meads Railway station, it was easy enough to research wartime France from books, of which there is no shortage. It's more difficult to know what to leave out, and how to sift through the mass of words to get the gems of information you need. This is where a synopsis wins hands down over the random storyline.

My researches led me to buy many second-hand books, but you will know by now that I am a collector. Also, they can be used again and again, and some will eventually be passed on to two of my grandsons, both keenly interested in wars and soldiering.

Aside from the romantic interests of my three Bannister sisters, I needed to know the progress of the war as a background, both to move my story along and to pace it.

World War 1 was a W. H. Smith book bargain that I bought for £6.50. Two sections in this book were of most use to me. One was 'War in the Air', and gave me much information regarding the flimsiness of those early planes. I also visited the Fleet Air Arm museum at Yeovilton, where I could see the actual size and dimensions of the planes.

The other section of most use in *World War 1* concerned women doing munition work. Through this, I discovered that women working with TNT had their skins discoloured yellow, and were known as 'canaries'. This was much too good a piece of information to waste! Illustrations showing the clothes the women wore in the factories were also helpful.

Many of the books I have bought in second-hand shops are new, and have presumably been remaindered by the publishers. One of these, bought for £2, was a large tome called *The First World War: Causes and Consequences*. The book covered the period from 1914 to 1938. It goes into vast detail, almost too much for my purposes, but also includes a brief rundown of the main events during those years, at home and abroad. This was only a rough guide, but was a useful backbone of chronology.

For actual day-to-day and month-by-month data of the war,

I frequently referred to the *Chronicle of the 20th Century*. Not only did this give newspaper-type reporting about the progress of the war from a military viewpoint, but many of the human interest touches, so essential in a novel but not always reported in a textbook. It was here that I learned about a London gang attacking a German baker in the streets in 1915, and the danger to foreign 'aliens' who had previously been part of the community - and this was also a situation I used in *The Bannister Girls*.

Fragments of information gleaned from many sources go towards the making of a novel, but you can spend ages reading reference books for perhaps the nugget of a few sentences. I've learned to skim the pages to find what I want - or think I may want. Perhaps this comes with practice - I only know it has saved me many tedious hours of wading through lengthy tomes! Anything that might be of use I jot down in a notebook, always noting the source book and page numbers.

Time-saving is partly the reason I will also look through the children's library, since the clarity of the explanations and the usual illustrations can save much time. Finding the basics in a children's book means you can often go straight to the index of a more detailed adult book for your needs, without fruitlessly poring over several hundred pages.

Further researches

I especially value illustrations in my researches, and one of my best finds, for which I paid £12, was a large hardback book called *What Did You do in the War, Daddy?*. It was also described as a visual history of propaganda posters, which were legion. Most of the posters in the book are British, Australian or American, but there are also German, French, Russian and more. They give a vivid and visual idea of how the countries reacted to urging people to enlist and to do essential war jobs. There were many sketches of army uniforms and civilian clothes, and details of work available to women, including a picture of a Land Army girl, which one of my Bannister sisters did become.

It's also worthwhile to buy books published in conjunction with television programmes. Some years ago Yorkshire Television produced a series called *How We Used to Live*. This, and the accompanying book, were written by Freda Kelsall, and has very useful domestic and social information covering the period 1902 to 1926. The illustrated chapter covering Britain at War mentioned Conchies – the conscientous objectors who refused to fight for various reasons – and one of these too figured in my book. He wasn't there just for 'local colour', but because he was important to one of the main characters. This reference book also told me about women in wartime, essential if I was going to involve Angel, Ellen and Louise in the war effort in some way, and this book also gave me more chronological data during those years.

When I subscribe to book clubs, it's usually for research books at bargain prices. In the Kings and Queens series published by BCA, my book on *The Life and Times of George V*, included the period from 1914 to 1918. Naturally, I looked up this section when researching *The Bannister Girls*.

It was in this book that I learned about George V's accident while touring the battlefields in France and Flanders. His horse reared in fright at the cheers from men of the Royal Flying Corps, and threw him, injuring him quite badly ... What an unexpected gem to discover, when my hero was an RFC officer ...

I never actually interviewed anyone for background reminiscences. This was not necessarily from choice. It just didn't occur. The Great War was a very long time ago, and sometimes memories can distort, and in this instance I felt I could obtain all that I wanted from other sources.

A friend loaned me a small journal that his soldier father had kept while in France during the war. While it said little about any military activity that could be of use to me, it revealed a great deal about the loneliness of the soldier at the Front. It also had a moving, and often vivid naïveté in the writing. Not that the man was a simpleton - far from it. But when someone faces possible death every day, feelings and emotions are very near the surface and are more easily written down on paper without inhibitions, and I felt that this was something I had to show in my novel.

For the human element of the novel, rather than the military, I found a small hardback book written in semi-diary form, called *Auntie Mabel's War* and laboriously sub-titled 'An Account of her part in the hostilities of 1914–1918'. The blurb inside the book ends with: 'Its charm lies in the sense of immediacy and period with which it illuminates one tiny corner of the Great War.' It does this admirably, giving a unique and often humorous insight into the way a young, middle-class girl coped with being a nurse during that war.

Letters to and from 'Auntie Mabel' also bore out the simplicity of expression in those days. Mabel's own education was reflected in her very correct writing. But many young men and women were suddenly away from home for the first time in their lives, and may never have put pencil to paper before. Rather than trying too hard to be literal in their writing, this resulted in the oddly charming openness already mentioned.

Auntie Mabel's book made fascinating research reading, detailing her life in France, and the memorabilia she collected. I was able to develop ideas from many of the illustrations. In fact, the cloisters of my fictional Abbey of St Helene gained inspiration from a photograph of Royaumont Abbey, which was used as a hospital during the war.

In any novel of love and war, terrible injuries and deaths will inevitably have their place. I needed no research other than memory to describe the anguish and courage of amputees, since such a tragedy had occurred in my own family through other circumstances. It's a fact of life that all experience is material for the novelist, however traumatic at the time – and it's often a peculiar kind of saving grace, allowing us to stand back, to observe and register, for a brief moment, before natural grief takes over once more.

Involving the characters

It's always a danger, when researching, to be so carried away by your knowledge, that you're tempted to include everything in your book. What results is not so much a novel as a glorified textbook. If that was their reading choice, people would go to the reference section of the library.

But novels are about people and what happens to them during the time span of your book, so it's important to centre the major factual activities around your characters, and not merely to write a long list of, say, wartime troop movements. There has to be a fine line between how much you include and how much you leave out. If you show only the tip of the research iceberg, you're in danger of writing a lightweight book. If you reveal every item you've discovered, you'll have bored your reader before she even gets to Chapter 2.

The secret is to involve your characters as much as you can in those recorded events, and to embellish them by creating fictional scenes of your own that can be taken to be authentic because they are based on fact.

The transition of time bothers many new writers. You may need to cover a period of time when things outside the domestic circle were making headline news, and need to be given due mention, even though they don't directly involve your characters.

I sometimes solve this by briefly listing events or dates of battles and so on in a single paragraph, then bringing my characters' involvement into the last event mentioned so that it finally focuses on them. Another way is briefly to list the various things that happened on a certain day, or month, and then include my character's movements on that same day at the end of the paragraph. Either way, the whole thing is given cohesion by this method.

If I want to let my readers in on some special aspect of the war, such as the Zeppelin raids or the effects of TNT on the skin of the girls working with it in the munitions factories, then it's much more effectively done through dialogue between the characters, rather than the author 'telling' it to the audience.

It's important to remember that you're writing a *novel*, and that readers are going to care about what happens to your characters. World events that don't directly affect those characters will be of only minor interest to readers. World events that *do* affect them should be researched as thoroughly as possible.

But if too much of your factual information is holding up the pace of your novel, you must discard it. However fascinating the facts you discover, if they are not part of, or add to, your story, then they become mere padding. Just as you skimmed the reference books for what you needed, so you need to skim your own writing at some point, to see if you're becoming long-winded and holding up the action.

One thing I avoided in my book was the overuse of slang terms. The way my people spoke depended largely on their backgrounds and local customs, and it seemed enough simply to avoid anything too modern. I didn't bring in any lines from well-known songs, although these always conjure up a time and place effectively, but copyright has to be observed. Instead, I invented song-lines of my own, where appropriate, in the style of the era.

The end result

At the time I wrote *The Bannister Girls* I considered it the best book I had written, and in many ways I still do. It was a departure from my other novels, so it was a challenge, and I didn't feel tied to the constrictions of a genre novel or any long-ago historical period. I became so immersed in the period that I felt the history and drama of it all around me as I wrote, and it was easy then to see events through my characters' eyes, and to experience their feelings.

I hope my enthusiasm showed in the writing, and in the joy I felt in those characters. I loved them all, even the ones I had to kill off. Finally, I felt that my own faith in the novel was justified when *The Bannister Girls* was shortlisted for the Romantic Novel of the Year award for 1990 from nearly a hundred entries.

It reached the final few ... and although it didn't win, it proved to me that the book you really want to write, the one you research thoroughly and are completely absorbed in, is the one that will bring its own rewards.

Sources relevant to this chapter

Books used in my researches

A Killing for the Hawks, Frederick E. Smith, Corgi, 1966.
Auntie Mabel's War, Marian Wenzel and John Cornish, Allen Lane, 1980.
Bristol as it Was, 1913–1921, Reece Winstone, 1978.
Chronicle of the 20th Century, Longman, 1988.
First World War, Causes and Consequences, The, Christopher Andrew, Systems Publications Limited, 1969.
How We Used to Live, 1902–1926, Freda Kelsall, Black, 1985.
Killing for the Hawks, A, Frederick E. Smith, Corgi, 1966.
Life and Times of George V, The, BCA, 1972.
Reaching for the Skies, Ivan Rendell, BBC Publications, 1988.
Von Richthofen and Brown, Joe Lavinia, Tandem, USA, 1971.
War in Three Dimensions, Air Vice-Marshal E. J. Kingston-McCloughry, Jonathan Cape, 1949.
What Did You do in the War, Daddy? OUP, 1983.
World War 1, Susanne Everett, Bison Books, 1980.

Places visited or remembered

Chateaux in France.
Fleet Air Arm Museum, Yeovilton, Somerset.
Temple Meads Railway Station, Bristol.
Vineyards in France.

Other

A soldier's journal.
All Quiet on the Western Front (film).

INDEX

INDEX